Photo by Eric Isselée

The song of the church mouse shall be heard in the land.

OF MICE AND MOOSE CALLS

Sonia Jones

OF MICE AND MOOSE CALLS

EP

Erser & Pond

Cover design by Benjamin Beaumont
Cover photos by Matt Keal (moose) and Oleg Kozlov (mice)

Printed in the U.S.A. by Erser & Pond Publishers, Ltd.
1096 Queen St., Suite 225, Halifax, N.S., Canada B3H 2R9

Library and Archives Canada Cataloguing in Publication

Jones, Sonia
Of mice and moose calls / Sonia Jones.

Illustrated in black and white. Also available in a colour ed.
ISBN 978-0-9810470-0-3

1. Jones, Sonia. 2. Canadian wit and humor (English). I. Title.

FC2345.L85Z49 2008 C818'.603 C2008-905574-8

10 9 8 7 6 5 4 3 2 1

First Edition

This book is dedicated to
Mom and Dad,
Gordon,
Valerie and Vicki,
Harrison, Alexa, and Danica.
I'll always love you.

CONTENTS

PROLOGUE

It is always a pleasure and a very great honor for an author to be invited to write a regular column for a respected publication with a wide and loyal readership. Such is *The Banner,* the denominational magazine of the Christian Reformed Church. When erstwhile editor-in-chief John Suk told me he was looking for some material that was both humorous and poignant, I jumped at the opportunity. During the first month of the turn of the century (this one, not the last one) my column, *Life Ever Laughing,* appeared in the pages of *The Banner.*

I hoped to provide my readers with stories that would make them chuckle over their morning coffee and also give them something to think about as they went about their daily business. Eight years have gone by now since the column's inception, so it seemed to me that it was high time to gather the stories together between two covers.

So here it is – a collection of topics ranging from warbling church mice to operatic moose calls, and from chaos on the farm to wild roosters running amok in the Dutch countryside.

But life has its darker side, too. You will come across poignant stories such as the one about a grieving linguistics professor, or a dog who sniffs out his owner's cancer. There is also a longer piece at the end of the book *(What's Wrong With My Baby?)* about my own daughter's brush with death.

It is my hope that you will take comfort in the knowledge that the tears will eventually be wiped away, and life at last will truly be ever-laughing.

I have changed the names of some of the characters to protect the privacy of the individuals who populate these true stories – with the notable exception of Obadiah Kelly, who is already so famous that it's useless to try to hide his identity. I'll bet you didn't know that his name is on your lips almost every day. Read on! There is much to learn.

Pipe organ photo by Marcus Lindström
Mice photo by Oleg Kozlov

And the song of the church mouse shall be heard in the land.

THE SONG OF THE CHURCH MOUSE

The last time our church offered a *Discover Your Gifts* workshop, my husband asked why we didn't balance it with a *Discover Your Faults* workshop. I thought it was quite an interesting idea. It would be enlightening to see ourselves as others see us, but what Gordon wanted was to hear himself as others hear him.

"I have a tin ear," he said. "I can't carry a tune to save my life. As far as I'm concerned, music is just a bunch of random notes."

"But Gordon," I said, "being tone deaf is not a fault. It's sort of like being color blind. You can't help it, so what could they really do for you in such a workshop?"

"Maybe they could sing the way I do and show me how I sound. I could learn by antithesis."

Later that night I was reading the newspaper in bed when I came across an arresting article about a naturalist called Juliet Clutton-Brock. She claims it's a well-authenticated fact that *mus domesticus,* the common house mouse, can sing. Apparently its song is like that of a warbling canary, only weaker.

What have I been missing? I have known some talented singers and musicians, and once I was even introduced to the great Luciano Pavarotti when he came to Halifax, but I have never had the honor of meeting a singing mouse of any description. Would Pavarotti ever consent, I wondered, to a romantic duet with *mus domesticus?* I suppose he'd have to sing with a chorus of at least a thousand mice, lest they be drowned out by his powerful voice.

I was bursting to tell Gordon about the article I had just read, but gentle snores were emerging from his side of the bed. I tried to sleep, but visions of mice with little top hats and canes kept dancing in my head. I cocked an ear toward the kitchen, hoping to hear some weak warbling sounds coming from the cupboards, but all I could discern was the hum of the fridge. Our condo isn't very mouse friendly.

But at our church I have seen clues in the dark recesses of the basement that suggest the presence of small guests of the rodent persuasion. I have never, however, heard their voices raised in song. I suspect they are too timid to mount a grand public performance.

Since I couldn't sleep that night I decided to get dressed and go to the church to see if the mice, in an unguarded moment, might treat me to a wee show. I let myself in through the front door with my key and tiptoed down to the basement, where I settled myself quietly on a discarded pew in the corner.

Time passed. Nothing happened. No church mouse choruses. Should I put out some tempting tidbits? I decided that a trip to the fridge would only encourage the mice to feast rather than serenade me. Besides, it would be better to remain as silent as possible lest they be too frightened to make their stage début with me lurking about somewhere in a dark corner.

I awoke with a start. The first rays of dawn were peeking in through some small windows up by the ceiling. My back was stiff. It seemed to me that in my head there lingered the last few notes of a low, canary-like warble. Had I been dreaming? I looked at my watch. Six o'clock! What would Gordon be thinking?

"It's true, Gordon, you've got to believe me," I pleaded, wondering how I would ever convince him that I had sneaked out in the middle of the night to hear some Christian Reformed mice singing at our church. I was perched on the edge of the bathtub watching him shave. It was difficult to analyze his expression under the white lather, but he had a hurt look in his eyes. Would he ever trust me again?

"I'm jealous," he said finally.

"You don't need to be."

"Those wretched little creatures can sing and I can't," he continued, lifting an earlobe to shave his jowl. "Are you going to tell me now that they sang *on key,* too?"

Birds sing, whales sing, and now it turns out that even mice can sing (having secretly attended, no doubt, some *Discover Your Gifts* workshops in their home churches). Solomon tells us that when the winter is over, flowers will appear on the earth and there will be a time of singing. In that day the tone deaf will surely lift their voices in perfect harmony with heavenly choirs of angels. And the song of the church mouse, too, shall be heard in the land.

Vatican photo by Slawomir Kruz
Moose photo by Greg Nicholas

I couldn't remember ever mentioning to Valerie that I was fond of moose calls.

MOOSE CALLS FROM THE ENGINE ROOM

My growing propensity to hear things incorrectly became painfully apparent to me when my husband, Gordon, and I went to Rome for a quick vacation. We were being squired around the Vatican by an ebullient Italian woman who was enthusiastically recounting the history of that landmark's famous paintings and sculptures.

I thought her explanations were excellent, but I was baffled by her frequent references to an engine room. What made her think that the engine room in the Vatican would interest the scholarly academics in our group? I asked Gordon for his take on our guide's comments about the Vatican's engine room.

He looked at me with a blank expression.

"She hasn't said anything at all about an engine room," he said, when at last he understood. "She's talking about *ancient Rome.*"

I comforted myself with the idea that my problem was based on my inability to understand certain accents. Gordon, however, soon disabused me of that notion. No sooner were we home again than I misinterpreted even what *he* had to say, and he has no discernable accent (at least to my ears). We were driving along the highway one morning, staring vaguely at the passing cars and discussing which type of vehicle we would buy when the time came to replace our old Volkswagen.

"*Beautiful Savior*," murmured Gordon.

I looked at him questioningly, but he had lapsed into what I assumed was a profound and prayerful silence. We had only just returned from the Vatican, after all, and who knew what sort of a spiritual renewal might have taken place in his heart while we were there?

"Yes, quite so," I agreed, feeling respectful of his thoughts on the matter. "Most interesting."

Gordon looked at me quizzically.

"You find it interesting?" he asked, trying to read my expression.

"Well, of course," I replied. "Why wouldn't I?"

"I never knew you had any thoughts one way or the other about the *Buick LeSabre*."

On January 1st I made a New Year's resolution not to misunderstand anyone ever again. That lasted till my daughter's boyfriend came to visit us from the Netherlands. Simon and I happened to be driving along together in the old Volkswagen (which had not yet fallen apart).

"Valerie says you like moose calls," he told me, right out of the blue.

I couldn't remember ever mentioning to her that I was particularly fond of moose calls.

"Yes," Simon insisted, "she told me you like them even more than opera."

"More than *opera!*" I exclaimed. "How could anyone like a moose call more than opera? Do you want me to imitate one for you?"

"Yes, please," he said, his eyes lighting up. He waited in eager anticipation.

I let out a terrific bellow that left Simon looking mystified and a bit crestfallen.

"It might not be the best moose call I've ever done," I said defensively, feeling slightly hurt that my earsplitting bawling had failed to impress him. "The truth is I've never actually heard one before."

"I don't understand," he said. "Valerie told me that you took her to the *Phantom of the Opera* just last year!"

I suddenly realized to my profound dismay that Simon must have thought I was a very untalented singer indeed – my imitation of a *musical* was no doubt the worst he'd ever heard.

With advancing age comes wisdom and the philosophical acceptance of reality in all its many guises. I no longer make New Year's resolutions. I have learned to live in a world where a beautiful Savior can be seen regularly rolling down the highways of the nation, and where the Pope himself can cock an ear in the middle of the night to hear an occasional moose call emerging from the engine room in the bowels of the Vatican.

I, for one, feel the richer for it. I'm certainly not ready yet to exchange the rather exotic pleasures of this brave new world for anything quite so mundane as a hearing aid.

Photo by Paul Mills

The Van Gelders explained to me that the kookaburra is an impertinent bird, known to the Aussies as "the laughing jackass."

STOP, KOOKABURRA!

Many of the trees in Australia are of the gum variety, known in North America as the eucalyptus. Among their long, leathery leaves dwells not only the renowned koala but also the kookaburra, a bird closely related to the kingfisher.

I first learned about the kookaburra in a song we used to sing at summer camp. Some of you might have heard it. We kids used to roast marshmallows around the campfire and sing in loud, confident tones about the kookaburra that sat in the old gum tree, eating all the gumdrops he could see.

"Stop, kookaburra, stop, kookaburra, leave some there for me," we bawled in enthusiastic cacophony.

Ten years later I finally laid eyes on a kookaburra in New York City, of all places. He turned out to be a nondescript gray-and-white bird who made his home (quite unwillingly, I'm sure) in the Bronx Zoo.

The placard by his cage described him as belonging to genus *Dacelo,* species *gigas,* and as being known for his peculiar cry. He was sitting drearily on the branch of an imitation eucalyptus, looking depressed and slightly moth-eaten. No amount of coaxing from his visitors could get him to demonstrate his peculiar cry.

For the next forty years I had the mistaken notion that the kookaburra was a taciturn bird with a jaundiced view of life, but a trip to Australia to visit my cousin Joan Van Gelder quickly set me straight.

I was awakened one morning by harsh, derisive laughter coming from the garden. It started out with a series of low "hoo-hoo-hoo-hoos," followed by a number of somewhat louder "hee-hee-hees," and ending in a strident crescendo with a full volley of "haa-haas." It was an eerie, triumphant cackle – one that left me clutching my husband's recumbent form as he lay peacefully sleeping by my side. I was sure that at any moment we'd be mercilessly attacked and left for dead by some terrifying marauder who was about to come crashing through the window.

"Halloy," my cousin Joan called out, knocking softly on the bedroom door. "I've brought you a spot of breakfast."

It was lunchtime before I had fully recovered from the shock of being awakened by the peculiar cry of the kookaburra. The Van Gelders explained that it's an impertinent bird, prone to amusing itself at the expense of unsuspecting people and known to Aussies as "the laughing jackass." Although it's a carnivore and feeds on caterpillars, fish, and frogs, it doesn't attack human beings (only their dignity).

To get my mind off my distressing early-morning experience, the Van Gelders kindly invited us to go to a sheep shearing demonstration. Just as we were walking down the path to the wool shed where the show was to take place, I was startled to hear a sheep bleating pathetically somewhere nearby. I turned to see if one of the animals had escaped from the paddock, but to my surprise there were no sheep anywhere in sight.

Suddenly I heard the bleating again, this time from just above my head.

What? Could one of the sheep have climbed a tree and gotten stuck?

I looked up into the branches of a gum tree and spotted a carella parrot watching me from between the leaves, his head cocked naughtily to one side. He had imitated the bleating of a lost sheep for the sheer enjoyment of watching my perplexity. Then, to add insult to injury, he gazed at me with an innocent expression and said, “Halloy,” in his best Australian accent. I felt like wringing his feathery little neck.

"Hoo-hoo-hoo-hee-hee-hee-haa-haa-haa-haaaa!" came the peculiar cry of a kookaburra from another branch of the tree. I was convinced he was laughing hysterically at my embarrassment. I was also sure that I saw the kookaburra wink at the parrot as they contemplated me from on high.

We humans are supposed to have dominion over the beasts of the field and the birds of the air, but the Australian versions of the animal kingdom have proven to be a bit of a challenge.

"Good on them," as the Aussies say.

To that I can only add that my trip to Australia taught me never to look down on the birds down under. They're smarter than I thought.

Photo by Emmanuelle Bonzami

I met Satan the other night, and I couldn't resist having a little fun with him.

MY BRUSH WITH SATAN

We all like to laugh in the face of danger. It comforts us to scoff at the things that go bump in the night. At Halloween some people even dress up as witches and goblins and hang skeletons on their doors. We like to represent Satan as a half-pint bully in red pajamas, laughing maniacally and brandishing a pitchfork. By minimizing evil, we somehow feel less threatened.

I do the same thing myself. Just the other night I met Satan, and I couldn't resist having a little fun with him. He was just as frightening as I had always imagined him to be, except that he wasn't wearing his red pajamas. He did have a tail, though, but it wasn't long and barbed like the ones in the familiar illustrations because Satan was a purebred Doberman pinscher.

"Sit, Satan!" bellowed the man next to me as we dog owners stood quietly in a circle with our canine companions at the local obedience school.

Satan's master was staring at him, pointing a firm finger at the spot on the floor where he wanted him to place his hindquarters. Satan was just about to obey the command when my own dog, Max, pounced on him, hoping to tempt him into having a little romp. Never one to resist an open door to deviltry, Satan was about to respond when his owner guessed what he had in mind.

"Sit!" his master barked in a thunderous tone.

I turned and looked at the Doberman, who under the authoritative gaze of his owner had deemed it prudent to ignore Max and adopt a sitting position. I bent down and asked Satan if he realized that his namesake had flunked out of obedience school, but I got no reply.

"Do you ever say to him, *Satan, get thee behind me?*" I asked his owner.

"No," he replied. "I just say, *sit!*"

Satan was definitely a dog to be reckoned with. He had a broad chest, fierce brown eyes, and teeth that went all the way down the back of his throat.

"How did you get him to show you his *teeth?*" said my little grandson Harrison when I told him all about Satan at dinner later that night. "Did you have to pry his mouth open with your hands?"

"No. Heavens, no. He yawned, that's all."

"Satan yawned?" he said, wide-eyed.

"Even Satan gets bored sometimes."

"What does he do when he's bored?"

"He likes to go around scaring people so he can see their horrified expressions. It gives him a sense of power. It makes him feel important."

We showed each other our very best horrified expressions until my husband, Gordon, reminded us that we were dining at an elegant restaurant and that it behooved us to act with decorum.

"Do you think Max was frightened of Satan?" Harrison whispered to me.

"No, I don't think so. He just wanted to play."

Vicki had rescued Max from a shelter when he was a puppy no bigger than the palm of her hand. He had grown up to be a rambunctious young dog with absolutely no talent at all for controlling his enthusiasm for life – which included a proclivity for clearing off the coffee table with his ever-wagging tail. Eventually I was recruited to take him to obedience school, where I had my brush with Satan.

"What did Satan sound like?" came Harrison's voice from somewhere under the table.

I lifted up the corner of the tablecloth, snarling and barking hideously.

"Sonia, *shhh!*" Gordon hissed. "The people at the table behind you are staring at you!"

"Don't worry," I said reassuringly. "Chances are they have children of their own. I'm sure they know what it's like to entertain a restless little boy."

"But Sonia," he said urgently, "they've only just been seated. They have no idea there's a little kid under our table!"

Later that night I got to thinking about my brush with Satan. Who, I wondered, has the last laugh in our close encounters with evil? We look for solace by poking fun at danger. We comfort ourselves by dressing Satan up as a little red devil. Might not that same devil derive satisfaction from our refusal to see him as he really is?

Fear is unpleasant, and we all try to avoid it by burying our heads in the sand. But fear is also a gift. It gets our adrenalin pumping in times of danger.

Without it, perhaps, we could die laughing.

Photo by Markus Drach

"There was a sign by the fence that said something about a *wildrooster.* I think it was a warning of some sort."

THE WILD ROOSTERS OF AMERSFOORT

My husband, Gordon, and I have long been considered honorary Nether-landers by our friends at church, who often refer to us as the Jonesmas. So last summer we decided that a visit to the homeland was long overdue.

"Are you sure we'll be able to find our way around?" Gordon said anxiously as we got ready to leave. "We don't know any Dutch."

"Don't worry," I said blithely. "Dutch and English are both Germanic languages. There has to be some connection somewhere."

"Do you think we'll be able to read the signs?"

"That should be easy," I answered confidently. "You'll see."

When we arrived at Schiphol Airport in Amsterdam, we rented a car and sallied forth to inspect the small country that had provided us with many delightful friends. Menno and Jani Boelens had kindly invited us to visit them in Amerongen, a little town to the southeast of Amsterdam. Utrecht lay directly in our path, so we decided to avoid that large metropolis by taking a route through a more rural area. We soon became hopelessly lost.

"Pull over here, Gordon," I said, as we wended our way through a small town. "I'll ask for some directions in that little store."

"Watch where you're going," he warned as I alighted from the car.

"It's okay. Look over there! They've painted the side of the road blue so the pedestrians can tell where they're supposed to walk. See, there's a sign over there that says *fietspad.* It obviously means *feet path.* It's easy to understand the signs."

As I trotted along the little blue path to the store, I felt inordinately proud of myself for my proficient translation of the road sign.

Then suddenly I was almost knocked down by a cyclist who came flying down the foot path at just under the speed of light. He shouted something unintelligible as he whizzed by.

"Young people today," I muttered to myself, glaring at him as he vanished over the horizon. "They'll ride their bikes anywhere."

After getting directions to Amerongen from the shopkeeper, I stepped onto the blue foot path again and headed for the car. This time I narrowly missed being bowled over by two different bicycles going in opposite directions.

"Some foot path," I complained to Gordon as I climbed back into the car. "I didn't know there were so many scofflaws in the Netherlands."

As the afternoon wore on, our progress toward Amerongen was severely impeded by the fact that no matter what road we took, we always ended up in the small city of Amersfoort. As if that weren't bad enough, once we entered Amersfoort the streets were all one way, and they led straight to the middle of town. One time we ended up on a street that came to a dead end at a canal, with steps leading invitingly down into the water.

"We're two hours late," I wailed. "Menno and Jani will be worried."

"I'm doing my best," said Gordon grimly.

Half an hour later, we were still in Amersfoort. We had arrived at a four-way stop where all the streets were one way and pointing to the middle of the intersection. After driving backward down the street we'd just taken and negotiating our way in and out of Amersfoort two more times, we finally found ourselves on a country road that seemed to be leading in the right direction. Or so we thought.

"If we're really driving toward Amerongen, why is the sun setting in the north?" I asked Gordon.

As neither of us could think of a satisfactory answer, I decided to get out and ask directions again at a nearby farm house. Gordon pulled over and I jumped out. Two minutes later I was back in the car again, slamming the door.

"What's the matter?" Gordon asked me, looking baffled. "You never went anywhere near the house. Aren't you going to get directions?"

"There was a sign by the fence out front that said something about a *wildrooster.* I think it's some kind of a warning. I don't want to get tangled up with any wild roosters!"

"Weird, these Dutchmen," Gordon mused as he drove down the road. "You'd think they'd come up with something a little more scary than a rooster for keeping trespassers off their land."

"Ask Menno. He'll be able to tell us."

"I can't ask Menno."

"Why not?"

"We're back in Amersfoort again."

We managed to save face by calling Menno and Jani from a store and inviting them to join us for dinner at an elegant little restaurant that we found near the canal in the center of Amersfoort. We dined on succulent trout with delicious dill sauce, then we spent the rest of the evening catching up on each other's news.

They were horrified when they heard that I had mistaken a bicycle path for a foot path. They tried hard not to laugh when I told them about the *wild-rooster,* which means *metal grate* in Dutch – something that is used to keep cattle from wandering.

The next morning was Sunday, so Menno and Jani whisked us off to their church. I listened carefully to the sermon to see if I could make sense of it. I soon recognized a word that sounded like *salmon.*

Shortly afterward I realized that the pastor was saying something about *hemel,* which I knew meant *heaven* in English (*himmel* in German). So! A sermon about salmon being served in heaven.

“Close,” said Jani. “Pretty close. But *samen* actually means *together* in Dutch. The pastor was talking about how some day we’ll all be together in heaven.”

I thought there was room for my interpretation, too. I like to imagine us all sitting at a heavenly banquet table (blissfully unthreatened by wild roosters and speeding bicycles), sharing pieces of beautiful fresh salmon that are even tastier and juicier than the ones we enjoyed in the restaurant in Amersfoort.

That’s assuming, of course, that we can find our way out of the city.

Photo by Karla Caspari

I decided to stand by the peephole until I caught Doris red-handed.

THE PILFERED PAPER

I am not in a particularly chipper mood until about 7 AM, by which time I've usually had my coffee and finished reading the morning newspaper. But for the past few weeks I've had to postpone all thoughts of feeling chipper until well after 9 o'clock, when the woman in apartment 703 finds it in her heart to return the paper that she "borrows" from our doorstep.

"How do you know it's Doris?" asked Gordon.

"She's the only one on our floor who doesn't subscribe to the paper."

"That's pretty flimsy evidence, I'd say."

In view of his remark I decided to stand by the peephole so I could catch Doris red-handed. But she must have had a trained fly posted on my wall, for our newspaper would inevitably disappear just at those moments when I happened to be buttering my toast or answering the phone.

A couple of days later I caught her *in flagrante.* There she was, crouched like a vulture over our morning newspaper, smiling beatifically at the prospect of being the first to discover what was going on in the world that day.

"Now she's got my wife lurking by the door and looking through the peephole?" said Gordon, when I told him how I had seen her grab our paper and dart back into her apartment.

"I think I should talk to her about this," I said.

"No, don't get into a fuss with Doris. Why not just call the circulation desk and have them tell the delivery person to push it under our door?"

It was a brilliant suggestion, and under normal circumstances the matter would have ended there. But I had seriously underestimated the strength of Doris's fingernails and her determination to prevail.

"You'll never believe this!" I said to Gordon the next morning. "That woman actually *scratched* the newspaper out from under our door! I'm really going to have to confront her this time."

"What's the good of that? You'll embarrass her. Anyway, she'll deny she took it, and *then* where will you be?"

The next day I called the circulation desk and asked them to deliver the paper to me at #708.

"Sorry, we can't do that. It says here that you live at #707."

"It's a double apartment," I explained. "The main door is #707, but #708 leads into the kitchen."

I felt quite certain that Doris would never want to take the chance of being seen scampering all the way from our kitchen door back to her apartment, clutching our newspaper to her bosom.

"We're not allowed to deliver your paper to the wrong address," said the clerk firmly. "It's company policy."

The next morning I waylaid the newspaper carrier and explained the whole thing again, asking him to deliver the paper to me at #708. He stared at me with wide, uncomprehending eyes.

"We live here, but that door down the hall is ours, too!" I said, wondering how I could get this across to him. It dawned on me that a picture is worth a thousand words, so I ran back through the apartment and flung open the kitchen door.

"See! This is our apartment as well!" I cried, waving to him down the hall.

"And a very good morning to you, too," he called back, with the hesitant, somewhat alarmed expression of a man who knows for certain that he is in the presence of mild insanity.

At that point I abandoned all hope of ever being the first to read my own newspaper. Gordon suggested I look for something else for us to read together over coffee. I scrounged around in the den and came up with *The Complete Idiot's Guide to the*

Bible, hoping it would provide some friendly advice for someone as idiotically helpless as I was.

The book turned out to be an intelligent, lively, humorous and yet insightful review of the Scriptures – one of the best summaries I've read in a long time.

Gordon and I now share some quiet time when we get up in the morning, and my chipper mood breaks through at the crack of dawn. As a matter of fact, we two old idiots are so pleased with our reading material that we are thinking of inviting Doris over to join us some day.

After she has finished reading our newspaper, of course.

Danger sign photo by Alicia Higgins
Art student photo by Beau Snyder
Chair photo by James Blinn

If it hadn't been for Professor Pita's electric chair, I might never have fully appreciated the beauty of Spanish art.

PROFESSOR PITA'S ELECTRIC CHAIR

If it hadn't been for Professor Pita's electric chair, I might never have fully appreciated the beauty of Spanish art. Toward the end of our class periods at the University of Madrid, our art history professor would call out a name from his student list. He would stare with a piercing gaze as his victim crept forward and sat on a straight-backed chair in the center aisle of the lecture hall. Then he'd dim the lights, turn on his slide projector, and the torture would begin.

"In which century was this painting created?"

The student would stare blankly at the slide.

"Is it from the medieval period?" he'd ask.

"No, it's too realistic. It has linear perspective."

"Well, was it painted during the Renaissance?"

"I don't think so."

"Why not?"

"Because you never give good tips so early in your interrogation."

Pita would persevere. He would loom over us, impervious to our fear, tormenting us with relentless questions.

"The appreciation of beauty does not just come spontaneously," he'd explain. "Without training, you cannot truly understand the subtle and complex aspects of the subject. Plato once said that *the contemplation of beauty enables the soul to grow wings.* It is my hope that your souls will someday grow wings."

Last February, for the first time in forty years, I returned to Spain. As I wandered through the Prado Museum I remembered how Professor Pita had generously allowed us students to celebrate the end of the academic year by putting *him* in the electric chair for a change. We asked him to analyze a depiction of "modern art" that we had painted ourselves, containing a hodge-podge of elements from many different times and places.

"Kindly identify the time frame in which this painting was created," we demanded.

"It is a work of the 20th century," he began.

"What about the Greek lintel?"

"It appears to be Corinthian, yet it is supported by an Ionic capital."

"And what do you conclude from that?"

"It is quite clear to me," he smiled, "that I am experiencing capital punishment!"

Now, as I toured the Prado Museum so many years later, I half expected to see Professor Pita come careening around the corner, fervently lecturing a new crop of students, but I knew it was just wishful thinking. He would be in his 70s by that time and he would have probably retired. Just then an elderly guard shuffled by.

"Excuse me, do you know a Dr. José Manuel Pita Andrade?" I asked him.

"But of course, Señora. He was the director of this museum for almost a decade. He is a man of extremely high standing in the art world. A *busy* man, too," he added, casting me a warning glance.

Later that evening I dialed the number that the guard had reluctantly given me. I was thrilled to be talking to Professor Pita again after so many years.

"What have you done with your life?" he asked, in his usual direct manner.

"I became a Spanish professor. It was you who inspired me."

"I feel moved by what you say. Now tell me -- have you discovered the essence of beauty?"

I paused as I pondered his question. Professor Pita had educated his students in the best sense of the word. He had inspired us to study our subject rigorously and to struggle with new and challenging concepts. The human spirit yearns to create beauty and to delight in its contemplation, but how does one understand the *essence* of beauty?

"Yes," I said finally. "And it was you who opened the door."

As Professor Pita so deftly demonstrated, the essence of beauty lies not so much in the artist's craft as it does in his ability to capture that ineffable quality that makes our spirits soar and for which we yearn with an almost painful hunger. Sitting in Professor Pita's electric chair and contemplating Spain's greatest pictorial and architectural masterpieces had been an experience that helped me to appreciate that truth.

Thanks to Professor Pita my soul, I knew, had grown wings.

Photo by Andreas Karetias

Sparkling like a sapphire under the fading sunset lay the majestic Agency.

A TURKEY IN TURKEY

"Are you crazy?" Gordon said, examining me over his glasses. "We got hopelessly lost when we went to the Netherlands last year, we got all tangled up with some notorious wild roosters, and now you're telling me you want us to go to *Turkey?"*

"Well, we're just a couple of old turkeys ourselves, so maybe it's time we saw how the other half lives," I suggested.

"You don't know a word of Turkish," Gordon snorted, returning his attention to the morning newspaper, which he had only recently managed to retrieve from our neighbor, Doris.

"Yes, I do! *Higher* means *no.* But I'm not sure how to spell it."

"Then, *higher,* we shall *not* be going to Turkey," Gordon said with finality.

We arrived in Istanbul on a pleasant September afternoon. We got lost only once along the way, in London's Heathrow airport, a cauldron of confusion teeming with angry-looking people determined not to miss their planes.

But in Turkey we found ourselves tucked safely under the fatherly wing of our tour director, Dr. Bastiaan Van Elderen, a dignified and sensible man in whom Gordon had complete confidence. He was a retired professor of New Testament Studies from Calvin Theological Seminary and had participated in several important archaeological digs. Gordon was relieved that we were being accompanied by a cheerful and circumspect group of seasoned CRC travelers with an infallible sense of direction and a no-nonsense attitude toward roosters, turkeys, and other assorted fowl.

"Did you know that Mustafa was a former *imam?"* remarked our Turkish guide, Selim, as he introduced us to the bus driver on the first day of our tour. "Yes, it's true. When he preached to the faithful everyone fell asleep, but now that he's a bus driver, everybody prays."

As a result of Dr. Van Elderen's well-informed lectures and Selim's laconic humor, we soon felt at ease in Turkey. We visited many interesting places such as the Archaeological Museum in Istanbul, the mausoleum of Attaturk in Ankara, Paul's well in Tarsus, the library at Ephesus, an ancient Christian church in Alahan which Bas had helped to excavate, and the ruins of six of the seven churches mentioned in Revelation.

When we arrived in Aphrodisias we decided to test the acoustics in the Roman theater by singing *"The Cross I Bear."* After belting out a rousing rendition of the hymn we began to disperse, feeling secretly quite pleased with our performance.

"What were they singing about?" a tourist asked his wife as we passed by.

"I dunno," she shrugged. "Something about a cross-eyed bear."

When we reached Antalya, Gordon and I had the pleasure of renewing our friendship with our Turkish "daughter," Ejbel Çira, whom we had hosted when she was studying marine law in Halifax, Nova Scotia. Since then she had joined the Turkish Coast Guard and was well on her way to a brilliant career. We were delighted that she could join our group for a couple of days.

"Now I show you the Agency," she said, at the end of our city tour of Izmir.

"The Agency?" I echoed, feeling most intrigued. I had visions of the Turkish CIA, or maybe the Turkish equivalent of the FBI. I was already dreaming of turning up the collar of my coat and lowering the brim of my hat as I walked stealthily down moldy hallways, stalking dangerous criminals.

This mysterious Agency would certainly be the highlight of our trip.

"We will see sunset over the Agency."

I thought it was charming that the Turks saw their spies and secret agents in such a romantic light. It had never occurred to me to visualize the CIA headquarters cloaked in a gorgeous sunset.

"Come! We must hurry," said Ejbel. "We go quickly before the sun disappears."

"I'm right behind you," I gasped, breathlessly trying to keep up with her.

"See? There it is! The beautiful Agency!" cried Ejbel, pointing triumphantly at the harbor.

As I followed the direction of her finger I beheld before me, sparkling like a sapphire under a fading sunset, the majestic Aegean Sea.*

* With the stress on the first syllable of "Aegean Sea."

Photo by Todd McLean

During drama workshop Mr. Dare made us do endless improvisations that put our believability to the test.

THE STANISLAVSKY METHOD

Our freshman drama class at Bennington College was taught by a young off-Broadway director named Michael Dare. In those days it was fashionable to teach aspiring actors to use the Stanislavsky method. The idea was that actors, to be believable, must get inside their characters by living and behaving as if they were one and the same person.

Bennington drama students were thus permitted to remain "in character" at all times. If we were training to play the role of a spy, we would put on sun-glasses and lurk in dark corners, surreptitiously taking notes on the movements of suspicious-looking professors. If we were learning to be shady dealers, we approached unsuspecting students and tried to persuade them to buy “brand name” watches at rock-bottom prices.

The operative word in the Stanislavsky method was “believable.” It wasn’t enough for us to convince ourselves that we were spies and shady characters – we had to convince Mr. Dare, too. During our drama workshops he made us do endless improvisations that put our believability to the test.

One day he decided to play an unsavory loan shark from the New York underworld. It was our job to explain to him why we needed his services and how we intended to pay him back. One by one we presented our cases, but he was not impressed.

“I don’t believe you,” Mr. Dare would say over and over in a gruff, raspy loan shark voice.

Finally it was my turn. I pleaded, reasoned, emoted, and even managed to weep one or two heart-wrenching tears, but the shark was having none of it.

"I don't believe you," he growled, dismissing me with a wave of the hand. "Next!"

That afternoon I knocked on his office door.

"How can I help you?" he asked me pleasantly, as I sat down by his desk.

I was in a terrible fix, I told him. That morning I had rammed my car into a cement post, so now I wouldn't be able to drive home for my mother's birthday. My savings didn't quite cover the damage, and if I made an insurance claim my parents would find out, so could he lend me some money until my next allowance?

"How much do your parents send you?" he said, hesitating.

"Enough to cover it, I promise."

"Well, I don't know. Don't you have any other friends you can ask?"

"I tried, but nobody else can help me. They're just students, like me. Oh, *please,* Mr. Dare!"

We stared at each other for a moment – I with pleading eyes, and he with a look that reflected the concerns of a young actor-in-residence who had probably not yet been paid for his first month on the job.

"Oh, all right," he said at last, opening a drawer and bringing out his check book. "I'm sure you'll pay me back."

"No, stop!" I cried, as he reached for his pen. "I don't need a loan. I just wanted to prove to you that I really am a believable actor, after all."

He gave me a wounded look that I'll never forget. My triumphant smile quickly faded and I sat twisting the sleeve of my sweater, too ashamed to look up.

Then in the terrible silence that followed, Mr. Dare suddenly started to laugh. It began as a series of labored wheezes that quickly reached a crescendo of deep, baritone hoots.

"I don't know if they're ready for you yet on Broadway," he said, contemplating me with the sort of generous, forgiving smile that no loan shark has ever smiled. "But you had me going, I'll say that much for you."

As I look back on our life at Bennington I'm touched by the patience and benevolence of the teachers who acted *in loco parentis* on that beautiful campus hidden away in the mountains of Vermont. We lived under the protection of some very gifted professors who loved us in spite of ourselves. But as in the case of our first parents in that other paradise, our hearts were not yet mature enough to return their love in kind. It wasn't until thirty years later that my own heart turned to the only God who is always believable.

And he doesn't have to use the Stanislavsky method.

Photo by Jeannot Olivet
Viruses by Sebastian Kaulitski

We forced the viruses to mutate back and forth between strains, as though we were playing a microscopic game of ping-pong.

KNOW THINE ENEMY

Predators are everywhere. They lurk in clever hiding places, they contemplate the world with narrowed, calculating eyes, they pounce when least expected, they ambush innocent passersby. Watch the nature programs. Predators are all over the place.

My job as a manufacturer of yogurt involves protecting some of God's tiniest creatures from their enemies. Any carelessness on my part can expose the yogurt bacteria to competition from hostile microbes that circulate in the air. If I let down my guard for a moment, unwelcome yeasts can settle gleefully on the surface of the finished product, replicating their spores with wanton abandon.

When I began making yogurt in the kitchen of our farm house 25 years ago, I knew nothing about the precarious existence of my diminutive protégés. I learned by trial and error. At first I was so unsuccessful in my attempt to produce marketable yogurt that my husband had to buy some pigs to eat my mistakes. They were uncritical admirers of all my abortive efforts, devouring the spoiled yogurt with flattering enthusiasm.

Eventually I learned the ropes well enough to take the next logical step: Gordon and I built a small factory close to the farm house. Everything went smoothly for several years.

Then one day I experienced what every yogurt maker dreads: a total batch failure. All three of our 400-gallon vats contained great clumps of white curds floating aimlessly in an ocean of yellow whey.

What could have gone wrong? I checked everything. No antibiotics in the milk. No chemical residue in the vats. The thermometers were correctly calibrated – yet the nightmare continued. Nothing but batch failures for the rest of the week!

We had a dairy consultant come to our factory to analyze our plight. After carefully examining the process and the product, he concluded that we had phage.

I stared at him. "Phage?" I echoed. I had never heard the word before.

"Bacteriophage," he said impatiently, as if he thought the longer word would clarify everything for me. "Viruses that kill yogurt bacteria."

"Well, how do we get rid of them?"

"You can't. You can steam clean the plant if you like, but some will always survive. They're here to stay. You're lucky you were able to get by as long as you did before they found you. You're pretty isolated out here in the country."

"Well, what do other dairies do?" I asked him.

"You'll have to change your bacterial strains every ten days or so. That way the viruses will have to mutate for about a week to get ready to attack, then you change to another strain and make them mutate again. When they're almost ready for the next assault, you change back to the first strain and so on. Just keep them confused. Make them mutate back and forth between strains as though you were playing a microscopic game of ping-pong."

We've been playing ping-pong ever since, and with gratifying success. But we've found it tedious, expensive, and irritating to have to protect our yogurt bacteria by keeping those miserable little viruses amused. I'd love to be able to just kill them off once and for all. There will certainly be a Nobel Prize waiting for the scientists who find a way to kill viruses, especially in the human host. It would be a triumph as great as the discovery of penicillin.

But wait! I read an article today in *The New York Times Magazine* about some microbiologists in a remote laboratory in Tbilisi who are using the phage virus itself to fight deadly bacteria that have become resistant to antibiotics. What a brilliant, creative new approach to curing diseases caused by bacteria that have "learned" to protect themselves against antibiotics! I suddenly felt ashamed of myself for secretly harboring such uncharitable thoughts about viruses – especially phage viruses.

Enemies are all around us, if we look closely enough. But perhaps we shouldn't be so quick to bring out the big guns. God entrusted us with the care of all his living creatures, so it behooves us to become better acquainted with the ones we consider to be pests or personal adversaries. Who knows, with a little love and nurturing and the occasional game of ping-pong, some of them might turn out to be our best friends.

Photo by Lisa F. Young

I was soon to learn that our days here on earth are not always a matter of life ever laughing. Sometimes our laughter is followed by tears.

CRY FOR ME, ARGENTINA

My favorite class in graduate school was Romance linguistics, taught by Professor Dmitri Chernovsky. I once asked him how many languages he spoke.

"My dear young woman," he replied. "I don't have my slide rule with me."

Professor Chernovsky was born in Moscow to a Ukrainian mother and a Russian father. His tutor was German, his nursemaid was Latvian, and the butler was Polish. The valet was of undetermined origin, and he spoke a language nobody knew. But Dmitri himself spoke no language at all. At the age of five he had not yet uttered a word. His mother had taken him to every specialist in Moscow, but nobody understood the cause of the child's silence.

Then one morning little Dmitri suddenly began speaking seven languages with astonishing fluency. His parents swept him into their arms and embraced him with tears of joy.

Dmitri couldn’t imagine what all the fuss was about. He had taken it for granted that fathers spoke Russian, mothers Ukrainian, nursemaids Latvian, tutors German, and so on. For the first five years of his life he had been quietly piecing together the components of this linguistic puzzle before finally bursting forth in exuberant speech.

Eventually he left home and traveled over four continents, mastering many more languages. His peripatetic life was capped off with a breathtaking romance in Argentina, where he met his future bride, María Elena de la Paz.

I might never have known Dmitri Chernovsky personally had I not chuckled out loud in his class one day. He was describing the etymology of an English word, tracing it back to its early origins.

“Today in modern English,” he said, “we have people going to the grocery store for food and sex.”

What? I stopped scribbling and peered at the other students. Their heads were bowed over their notepads as they took down Professor Chernovsky’s remarks. Not one hand was raised, nor indeed were any eyebrows. I stole a glance at the notes of the student next to me. “People go to stores,” he had scrawled, “for food in sacks (from Latin *saccus,* Greek *sakkos,* Hebrew *saq.*).”

Later Professor Chernovsky asked me to explain the reasons for my ill-concealed amusement. This eventually led to a discussion over coffee about some of the finer points of phonology. We shared many enjoyable “accent” jokes, but I was soon to learn that our days on earth are not always a matter of life ever laughing. Sometimes our laughter is followed by tears.

That night I was jangled awake by the phone. A doctor informed me that my father had died of a coronary occlusion. I was shocked, and I wept inconsolably until daybreak.

The next morning people were walking along the streets, hurrying to work and acting as if nothing had happened. *But my father had died.*

I had not yet heard that there would be a time when our tears will be wiped away, so I went to Professor Chernovsky's office, seeking comfort. I recalled how he had left his family at a young age. How had he coped?

"Some people find solace in letters or old photo albums," he said. "As for me, I'm reminded of my loved ones when I hear their languages. If someone speaks Russian, I think of my father. And when I hear Ukrainian, I remember my mother." He gazed at me sadly, searching my face. "Do you know the *vos* form they use in Argentina?" he asked.

"I'm familiar with it, yes."

For the rest of the hour he spoke in the musical Spanish peculiar to Argentina. The cadences were beautiful and strangely consoling.

It wasn't till after my final exams that I learned that Professor Chernovsky's wife had passed away just a few days before my father. He had hidden his pain from me in his office that day so I'd be free to express my own sorrow.

I felt a wave of regret. I had been so immersed in my own misery that I hadn't noticed his unspoken grief. Later I remembered the flowing, silvery tones of the *Río Plata.* Professor Chernovsky's voice had grown soft as he sought to restore my spirits. He had spoken reassuringly in that musical Argentine Spanish, showing charity to a young student he hardly knew, while he himself took silent comfort in the language of his Argentine bride.

Photo credit Stock Photo NYC

A rose by any other name would indeed smell just as sweet to an unprejudiced nose, but a good nose is hard to find.

NOSES AND ROSES

A rose by any other name would indeed smell as sweet to an unprejudiced nose, but a good nose is hard to find. Most of them are strongly influenced by verbal descriptions of the odors that go wafting past their olfactory nerves. No advertising executive, for example, would ever dream of using an adjective normally associated with raw sewage to describe a new perfume. It wouldn't take much to persuade her that nostrils in the target market would flare in disgust at the thought of being exposed to a scent with such a label.

The same can be said of taste buds. They, too, depend heavily on verbal descriptions to guide them, often refusing to let their owners sample any kind of food that lacks an appealing name.

Yogurt is a case in point. Although the word *yoghurti* rang pleasantly in the ears of the ancient Turks, modern consumers tend to recoil at the name. When I try to hand out free samples of my yogurt in the stores, I am met with suspicious looks and noses wrinkled in disgust. If people could close their nostrils as camels do, they would clamp them tightly shut in these situations.

"You're not going to get *me* to eat that stuff," I am told with great finality by passing shoppers. "I don't even like the sound of the word."

"Which syllable do you dislike the most, '*yo*' or '*gurt*'?" I ask them.

"Both," they invariably reply.

"Would you still hate yogurt if it were called *barbecued steak*?"

"Probably," they say as they turn and scamper away, holding firmly onto their children who frown over their shoulders at me with the expression of a kid who has just been saved by an alert mom from the wiles of a malevolent stranger. It's obvious to them that I'm up to no good.

Now don't look down your nose at those biased taste buds and intolerant nostrils that I have just described. There's worse to come. Eyes have their blind spots too. I once had a job interview with a professor at a small college. When we were just five minutes into the interview, he sat back in his chair and studied me with narrowed eyes.

"You don't look like a Spanish teacher to me," he announced, right out of the blue.

"What does a Spanish teacher look like, then?" I asked, with genuine curiosity.

"I don't know," he replied.

"Then how do you know I don't look like one?"

He became defensive, changed the subject, and brought our conversation to a sudden close. It was the shortest and most bizarre interview I've ever had. It was becoming clear to me that perception is everything.

My conclusion was corroborated years later by some remarks my oldest daughter made one day after attending a writers' conference.

"You'll never be an important author, Mom," she said. "You don't act like one, that's why. The writers at the conference were so unapproachable. They acted as though they were much too important to talk to. But you're not scary enough, Mom. You should develop a persona. You should wear spike heels and lots of jewelry and a broad-rimmed hat and sunglasses. You need to package yourself, or nobody will ever take you seriously."

I sighed. Marketing has taken over the world, and perception has become reality. Impressionable eyes, ears, noses and palates have fallen victim to current fashions and manipulative media executives. But perhaps it was ever thus.

"You don't look like a king," they said to him in Jerusalem over two millennia ago, gazing dubiously at the modest, unassuming Galilean. Didn't anyone ever tell him that a white stallion would have been a better advertising tool than a scruffy little donkey? Couldn't somebody take him aside and show him how to package himself more effectively? Some spit curls on his forehead, like those of the great Caesar, might have been a good place to start. And why couldn't he adopt Caesar's haughty expression, instead of looking like a man of sorrows, acquainted with grief?

A woman came forward and tearfully washed his feet with expensive scent that had the fragrance of roses in the early morning dew. Noses twitched. To some of the onlookers the perfume smelled like money down the drain, and they murmured bitterly among themselves. But to the gentle, melancholy Messiah the gift was a harbinger of the day when the lame man would leap as an hart and the eyes of the blind would see.

Photo by Igor Burchenkov

Obadiah Kelly is the most famous man who ever lived, yet nobody has ever heard of him.

OBADIAH KELLY

Obadiah Kelly is the most famous man who has ever lived. His name is on everyone's lips (even yours) many times a day, and yet nobody has ever heard of him. I didn't know who he was either until my friend Ping asked me about him one evening during our English lesson. Ping is a young physician from a farming community in China, and even the people in her village refer to this individual on a regular basis. But like everyone else in the world, they use only his initials.

"What do the letters *O.K.* stand for, anyway?" she wanted to know.

I gave her a blank stare.

"I have no idea," I confessed.

"In China it's very popular to say *O.K.*" We all thought it was an American expression."

I went to the bookshelf and pulled out my *Dictionary of Word Origins* by Joseph T. Shipley. He advanced several theories describing possible sources of the word, but the one Ping and I liked best involved a reference to Obadiah Kelly, an early railroad clerk who initialed all the parcels that he accepted for forwarding.

Our imaginations ran wild. Did Obadiah Kelly have any idea that everyone in the whole world would eventually be using his initials to indicate agreement or satisfaction? Where did he live? Ping thought he might have been from a rural area where people were simple and straightforward, and that fame would have been rather embarrassing for such a man.

On the other hand, maybe Obadiah was bored with his life and nursed a secret ambition to be well known. Perhaps he had made a pact with the Devil in an unguarded moment, conveniently forgetting his pastor's sermon about how the Enemy promises everything and delivers nothing.

It would be just like Satan to assure Obadiah Kelly that his name would be spoken the world over, while at the same time neglecting to mention that only his initials would be used. He'd couch his promise in words that were familiar to Obadiah but which placed the situation in a totally different light. The suggestion would be that people of all nations and all tongues would sing his name in one voice.

How could Obadiah Kelly not visualize, with ill-concealed self-satisfaction, the swelling crowd and the majestic singing? He would never confuse himself with the Godhead, of course – not a humble man like him. But would it not be delightful to hear his name on the lips of such vast numbers? He wouldn't *be* God, but he would be *like* God. What an enriching life experience! Why had that thought never occurred to anyone else?

"And how soothing for your wobbly self-esteem," Satan would hiss, coiling himself around Obadiah's knees and fixing him with a magnetic gaze. "I'll make your name stand for harmony and friendly agreement. Who could ask for more?"

Obadiah Kelly smiled dreamily. He would be a man to be reckoned with. Now maybe even *Mrs.* Kelly would admire him and look up to him at last.

The railroad clerk was just about to sink his teeth into the apple when my husband passed by on his way to the kitchen to see if anything tasty had materialized in the fridge since his last visit.

"What are you two chuckling about?" Gordon asked, glancing curiously at Ping and me.

"We were talking about Obadiah Kelly," I said.

"Who's he?"

"Oh, just some guy who worked for a railroad company long ago. Nobody knows anything about him, so we were trying to imagine what he might have been like."

Gordon closed the refrigerator. “I’m going to take this last piece of key lime pie, O.K.?”

“Go ahead. It’s Obadiah Kelly with me.”

“Who? Oh, the railroad clerk.” He frowned. “Should Ping really be wasting her time studying an unknown character like him?” he asked as he turned away. “Wouldn’t she be better off learning about somebody *famous?”*

Photo by George Peters

Demonstration of the correct installation of the author's conception of a wall switcher

BREEDING CHAOS

I am not sure that it pays to study linguistics. Granted, missionaries have spread the good news in every known language, and wonderful things have been accomplished by translators who have made the Bible available to readers all over the world.

In my case, however, the emphasis on phonology seems to have left me with a propensity to attend to the sound rather than to the meaning of words. This has opened the doors to a perplexing wonderland of bizarre misunderstandings.

Just the other day I was chatting with our next door neighbor, Travis Oickle, a kindly farmer who has always given us excellent advice about mending fences, tedding hay, making straight windrows, and rounding up wayward bovines.

"Are you going over to the volunteer firemen's dance?" he asked me.

"No, I'm afraid not."

"Too bad," he said, looking a bit downcast. "I wanted a wall switcher."

"A wall switcher?" I said, brightening. "Maybe Gordon can be of some help."

I was so pleased to be able to do something for Travis in return for all the assistance he had given us around the farm that I failed to notice his puzzled expression. I assumed that a wall switcher was a piece of electrical equipment of some sort, and I knew that my husband had plenty of that kind of stuff lying around in the shed.

"A wall switcher?" said Gordon at the supper table that night.

"Yes, that's right. Travis says that the volunteer firemen need it at the dance hall. Maybe it's a light dimmer or something, to make it more romantic."

Gordon suddenly saw the light.

"He must have been disappointed when you told him that maybe *I* could help him out," he chuckled. "He wasn't asking for a wall switcher. He wanted a *waltz with you!"*

My linguistic affliction flared up again in Australia when we were attending the 23rd World Congress of the International Dairy Association. The organizers had arranged for us to visit a local dairy farm, and I was enjoying the tour.

"Do you have chaos on your farm?" the owner asked me, as we walked toward the milk barn.

I was convinced that he had taken one look at me and deduced that any farm with which I was even loosely associated would inevitably suffer from its fair share of turmoil and confusion.

"Oh, yes," I admitted, smiling bravely. "But my husband is good at handling all the problems."

"Is that so?" he replied, giving me a quizzical look. "And how many chaos does he milk?"

I decided then and there to concentrate my efforts on the *written* word so as to avoid any further misunderstandings. To this end I gladly accepted the job as bulletin editor for our church, secure in the belief that I would function well in that position.

One day I got a phone call from a deacon who informed me that the evening collection was for the Netherlands Fund. When the congregation read the news the next Sunday, they were baffled by this Netherlands Fund. It seemed to them that the Dutch homeland was a prosperous nation and not exactly in need of financial aid. The mystery was solved when I asked the deacon to clarify the matter.

"Not the Netherlands Fund!" she exclaimed. "I said *Benevolence Fund!*"

I live in a world where wall switchers lurk in dusty sheds, where Australian farmers love to breed chaos, and where the Dutch have a special fund for dark and mysterious purposes. With my higher-than-average capacity for linguistic mix-ups I've decided that the safest place for me is to be alone in the pasture, watching the cows chew their cud.

I've developed quite a talent for imitating their bellows. They generally stop in mid chew and gaze at me with all-too-familiar expressions of mystified bewilderment. I don't dare to ask myself what they think I'm saying, but I'm hard at work these days applying linguistic principles to an interpretation of their responsive moos. I hope my efforts in this direction won't lead to any particularly distressing misunderstandings between us. I already have enough trouble with the chaos in my life.

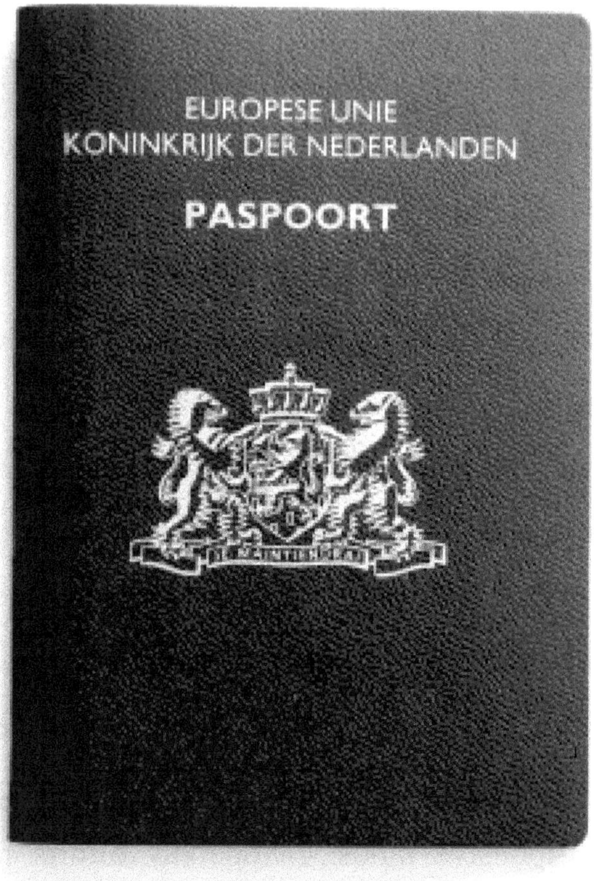

Photo by Ruud de Man

Jesus must have felt incredibly frustrated when he told people who he was and they wouldn't believe him.

ID, PLEASE

Jesus must have felt incredibly frustrated when he told people who he was and they didn't believe him. They usually got it all wrong. They murmured, misinterpreted, and mangled the information. Was he Moses? Elijah? A liar? A lunatic, maybe? They figured they might as well stone him and be done with it.

I've had a number of problems, too, with people misconstruing my identity, so I can relate (at least on some levels). Back in the early '70s I attended my first academic conference. I was proud to be sporting a name tag identifying me as a member of the *Canadian Association of Hispanists*. I was a neophyte specialist in Hispanic studies, and now here I was, rubbing shoulders with the luminaries in my field.

That night in the hotel I was in the elevator with a bellhop who kept staring at my name tag.

"Are you hypnotists going to put on a magic show?" he asked, his eyes bright with anticipation.

As I left the elevator I tried to explain to him that a Hispanist has very little in common with your average hypnotist, but the door closed and the bellhop disappeared.

Some years later I approached a young cashier at the checkout counter in a quiet store. She had been whispering and giggling with another sales clerk when I put my purchases on the counter, but her expression grew serious when she read the name on my credit card.

"What are you a doctor *of?*" she asked, peering at me with friendly curiosity.

"Romance languages," I replied, somewhat defensively. I was quite certain that she wouldn't be interested in hearing anything about languages deriving from Latin. She was probably hoping I was a brain surgeon or at least a medical specialist of some kind.

"You're kidding! That's *awesome!*" she said, nudging her friend.

Great, I thought. *That's all I need. A sarcastic sales clerk.*

"Listen," she said, leaning forward and talking in confidential tones, "if you have the time, maybe you can help me. I've got this boyfriend, see, and we've been having some trouble lately..."

But nothing can match the frustration I felt just the other day when I was walking around in the Farmers' Market with a collection of yogurt samples on a tray. My husband and I had begun making the product 25 years ago with the excess milk of our cow, Daisy. Eventually our company became the leading yogurt producer in the Maritime Provinces. Later, however, we experienced heavy pressure from the multinationals, so we decided to hand out free samples at the popular Farmers' Market where we could meet some of our customers face to face. Everything went smoothly until I was confronted by an irate farmer.

"You shouldn't be calling yourself by that name," he growled, pointing an accusing finger at the logo on my T-shirt.

I looked down at my chest, wondering what could be offensive about the name *Peninsula Farm* with a picture of Daisy grazing by a barn.

"You're using the very same logo they've got on the yogurt containers in the supermarkets," he said indignantly.

The light finally dawned.

"But that's *my* company!" I explained.

"I don't mean *this* yogurt," he said, indicating my tray. "I'm talking about the yogurt they sell in the *supermarkets.* You shouldn't be using their name. It's not right, you know. You shouldn't copy them. They could sue you."

"But I own the company that makes the yogurt in the supermarkets."

"Shame on you. I'm not stupid. They're a *big* company. You'd never see *their* president walking around here with a tray."

Jesus had heard it all before. The real Messiah would never dream of associating with *hoi poloi* in the market. The people were onto him. They told him he should be ashamed of himself for making false claims about who he was.

The farmer stood with his hands on his hips, frowning at me as I walked away.

Hypnotists of the Miss Lonely Hearts variety who pretend to be big-time yogurt moguls can get into a lot of trouble. I looked back at the scowling farmer and smiled sheepishly.

At least he didn't throw any stones.

Photo byWilli Schmitz

"Ain't no use gettin' a growed-up bull," Travis said. "When they gets big, they's nothin' but trouble in a leather bag."

EDUCATING GORDON

When God told Adam and Eve to be fruitful and multiply, he said nothing at all about choosing the gender of their offspring. This never seemed like much of an issue to Gordon and me until we moved to a small farm in Nova Scotia to escape from our hectic, stressful life in Manhattan.

We arrived with three suitcases, ten cartons of books, the financial proceeds from the sale of Gordon's management consulting business, a case of diapers, and one baby girl – not necessarily in that order of importance. Our property lay stretched out along half a mile of ocean frontage, green and inviting against the cool water. We fully expected to settle into a quiet life of serious scholarship and languorous days of sailing.

Our neighbor, however, had other plans for us. At first Travis was too shy to come over and say hello. He had heard from the grapevine that a professor had bought the adjoining farm and he was afraid he would feel intimidated by such an exalted personage. But when he learned that the professor was only me, he quickly befriended Gordon and offered to give him some pointers about running the farm.

"It ain't my place to tell a man what to do," Travis said shyly. "But you fellows needs to get some critters to gnaw off the land, or it'll go back to alder bush."

Gordon had no idea what type of critters Travis was talking about. Being from New York the thought of cockroaches came to mind, but Travis quickly divested him of that notion by taking him to an auction where he helped him pick out some beef cows along with a mild-mannered little bull whose growth potential had yet to be achieved.

"Ain't no use getting' a growed-up bull," Travis remarked, in answer to Gordon's inquiring glance. "When they gets big they's nothin' but trouble in a leather bag. But you won't have no problems handlin' this young lad here. It don't matter none if the critter's young or old, the seed's still the same."

"But do you think he's he tall enough to reach the cows?" Gordon asked dubiously.

"We'll hoist him onto a milk stool," Travis replied, without cracking a smile.

By the following spring I was pregnant again and our meadows were dotted with calves. Gordon leaned against the fence, happily surveying what God had wrought.

"They look so clean and new, don't they?" he said. "Look how white their patches are."

"Maybe so, but you ain't looked underneath," Travis replied. "Them's all bull calves you got there. Guess you'll be havin' a veal sale in the fall."

"You mean I have to *kill* them?" said Gordon, looking dismayed.

"What else can you do with 'em?" Travis asked. "Them's no good as pets."

"I'm going to become a vegetarian, then."

"That won't solve no problems. If you don't beef them critters you'll end up with bulls all over the place. Next thing you know they'll be runnin' loose in the streets of Lunenburg, scatterin' the women and chargin' into things."

A few weeks later Gordon brought me home from the maternity hospital where I had given birth to our second daughter, Vicki. When Travis saw our car come up the drive, he ambled over to the house to take a look at the new arrival.

"Gordon," he sighed, shaking his head and looking disapprovingly at the baby. "You hasn't learned very much, if you don't mind me sayin'. Farmers is supposed to have *sons,* and if you wants to increase your herd, what you needs is *heifer* calves. You city folks seem to get everythin' all turned around backwards."

Nowadays I shudder when people tell me how easy it is to use the latest medical technology to select for gender. I think about Travis and his disturbingly practical approach to life. No wonder God didn't mention the subject to Adam and Eve. They were about to cause enough trouble as it was

Exclusive to istock photo

"Stars and planets are always where they belong," Sheila said. "That's why I like to think about them."

A STAR FOR SHEILA

If my husband, Gordon, hadn't been taking a course on celestial navigation, we might never have appreciated the true extent of my sister's special gift. We were at my mother's house for a weekend visit and Gordon had brought along a stack of books to study for his exam.

"These practice questions are killing me," he groaned.

My sister Sheila looked up from her tatting.

"What's the problem?" she asked.

"They expect me to know where Venus would be if I were in Buenos Aires on February 13, 1938, at 5:00 in the morning."

"It would be in the constellation Aquarius."

Gordon stared at her. "You're kidding, right? You can't possibly know that without looking it up in the almanac."

But Sheila wasn't kidding. She had memorized the almanac.

My mother knew that Sheila was "unusual" ever since she was a little girl. For one thing, she tended to echo what people said, rather than using language as a means of communication. She loved repetitive tasks, and she became easily frustrated if anyone interrupted her.

Over the years she developed a personal daily routine, and woe betide anyone who attempted to change it! She was particularly gifted at performing tasks that required excellent hand-eye coordination. She won many prizes for her intricate weaving, and she once crocheted a 14-foot altar cloth that was the envy of the local Catholic community.

I knew Sheila had a phenomenal memory, but I never realized it was of encyclopedic proportions till the day she told Gordon about Venus. When I asked her why she had bothered to memorize the entire almanac, her answer was simple.

"Stars and planets are always right where they belong," she said. "That's why I like to think about them."

Sheila wanted her life to be completely orderly and predictable, so she focused all her attention on studying the stars and creating complex designs for her loom. She had little interest in the chaotic ebb and flow of human affairs, and was unsuccessful in her attempts to fit herself into the workaday world. She ended up living at home with my mother, where she was free to enjoy her routine.

My mother ran the household, as Sheila found it hard to concentrate on matters that were peripheral to her own agenda. Although I suspected that Mom might have felt trapped by the responsibility of Sheila's long-term care, she never complained. She had been a widow for many years and was probably glad for some friendly conversation, even if it did focus primarily on astronomy and fabric design.

As time went by my mother's memory started to fail. It began with her short-term memory and then moved insidiously backward over time so that she found herself grieving the death of my father, then celebrating the birth of her children, then joyfully preparing for her wedding. Eventually she recalled only the early days of her childhood in Alaska.

Gordon and I visited from Canada whenever we could. My mother was a gracious hostess even though she didn't recognize the two rather bold strangers who behaved as if they were members of the family. We were prepared to arrange for professional care if the situation warranted it, but to our delight and relief Sheila rose to the occasion and began to learn how to take charge. Thanks to her prodigious memory she never needed to make a shopping list or remind herself to pay the bills. What's more, her unusual personality was ideally suited to patiently answering my mother's repetitive questions. Through God's loving provision, an autistic woman had been equipped with the special talent to care for an aging mother with Alzheimer's.

Some years later my mother died quietly in her sleep. During the funeral I noticed that Sheila was making the sign of the cross.

"Do you remember Father Louis, the priest I made the altar cloth for?" she asked me. "Well, he's been visiting Mummy and me for more than twenty years now. Toward the end, Mummy had some trouble remembering what he taught us, but she believed in God and so do I. He's in charge of the universe. That's why the stars are always where they belong. We both like it that way."

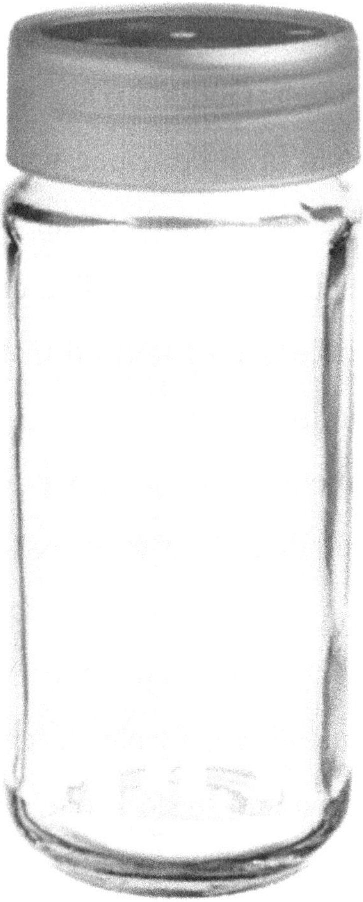

Photo of jar by Markus Guhl
Moonbeams by Benjamin Beaumont

"Would you rather swing on a star,
Or carry moonbeams home in a jar…?"

A JARFUL OF MOONBEAMS

When I was a child I not only spoke as a child, but I used to sing a song that captured my imagination in a big way. Some of you may remember it:

Would you rather swing on a star,
Carry moonbeams home in a jar,
And be better off than you are,
Or would you rather be a…?

As an alternative to the exciting possibilities described in the first three verses, you were offered the chance to become a rather dreary, earthbound animal such as a pig or a fish. I couldn't imagine why anyone would ponder the second option even for a moment.

Today's astronomers and astrophysicists must feel the same way. Outer space is filled with opportunities to let your imagination run wild. I'm constantly reading stories about wormholes leading to other universes or about what life might be like in dimensions proven to exist by formulae devised by theoretical mathematicians. But these days it looks as though reality is becoming stranger, and far more worrisome, than fiction.

Yesterday my friend, Daniel Walker, told me about a BBC news report he'd read on the Internet. Apparently a team of scientists has announced that mankind will soon have the ability to move the Earth into a new orbit.

"They seem to think we're a little too close to the Sun," Daniel explained, "so they'd like to make a bit of an adjustment."

"Just how do they intend to change our orbit?" I asked him.

"They're talking about using the gravitational slingshot technique that already sends space probes to the outer planets. They don't mention exactly how they would do this, but one gets the impression that they intend to snag a passing asteroid with a sort of cosmic lasso."

"And why would they want to do that?"

"Well, they say that this would help the Earth to maintain a benign climate as the Sun increases its luminosity over the next billion years."

"It's like using a cannonball to kill a mosquito, and *we're* the mosquitoes!"

"The thing that gets me," said Daniel, "is the amazing *hubris* that becomes evident in the article. One of the astronomers was quoted as saying that the technique they're developing for repositioning the Earth is alarmingly feasible."

"Alarming is right," I said. "Engineers can't plug the leaks in our condo building, but they want to change the Earth's orbit! How scary is *that?*"

"Tell me about it. There was a time when astronomers were talking about 'terraforming' Mars to make it more like Earth so we could live there comfortably, but now they're saying that the Earth-orbital-migration technique is a much easier way to provide living space for humans in a changing solar system."

"But the concept is laughably dangerous," I objected. "If you change the Earth's orbit then you'll destabilize the orbits of other planets, and who knows what could happen then? I shudder to think. Plus if the slingshot procedure just happens to cause the asteroid to collide with the Earth, it's curtains for all of us!"

"You don't have to convince *me,*" said Daniel, with a rueful smile.

I didn't know whether to laugh or cry. Our imaginations are fired by the heroic notion of going boldly where no man has gone before, but in the back of my mind I could hear the quiet chortle of the serpent. He fools many of us into thinking that if we decline his kind offer to play God with the universe, we're automatically opting to be nothing more exciting than a pig or a fish.

When I was a child I quite naturally dreamed of carrying moonbeams home in a jar. I still entertain poetic visions, but they're of a different sort. Now that I see through the glass of my adulthood (albeit darkly), I look forward to the dawn of God's new heavens and his new earth. In that day we'll be too busy drinking it all in to even *think* of interfering with the orbits of his heavenly bodies.

The priest in the intelligent musical, *Man of la Mancha,* said it well:

> *For if you build your life on dreams*
> *it's prudent to recall*
> *A man with moonlight in his hands*
> *has nothing there at all.*

Maranatha.

Photo by Patti Calfy

The serpent was lucky he didn't have to argue with the tough-minded Miss McGraw.

THE WINSTON FALLACY

There was a time when grammarphiles were alive and well and working busily in their natural habitat, the English class. As a species these grammar lovers were known as "Miss Grundy," but it's unclear how the surname became associated with the study of grammar. Some say the name is an onomatopoeia describing the disgruntled noises made by schoolteachers who are overexposed to grammatical errors. Others insist it's a corruption of the word "grumpy," which is how teachers must feel when they grapple too long, and often in vain, with sloppy speech habits.

As a schoolgirl I would never have realized that grammarphilia extended well beyond the confines of the classroom had it not been for an advertising campaign put on by R. J. Reynolds, the tobacco company. Their TV commercial featured a chorus line of long-legged dancing girls brandishing giant cigarette cartons and exuberantly singing, "Winston tastes good, like a cigarette should."

The warbling, winking girls got a reaction that the marketing team over at R. J. Reynolds hadn't anticipated. Grammarphiles who had previously lain dormant suddenly came to life and took to the streets in droves, complaining bitterly about the deplorable use of English in the Winston jingle. Indignant citizens sent letters expressing their outrage to the corporate offices in North Carolina. Newspaper editorials bemoaned the use of bad grammar and the appalling influence this had on American youth. If there was a cautionary word expressed here or there about the dangers of tobacco itself, nobody heard it in the midst of all the outrage.

The marketing boys at R. J. Reynolds couldn't believe their good fortune. They got right to work on a new TV ad, showing a grimacing, prune-faced schoolmarm teaching her students to say, "Winston tastes good, *as* a cigarette should." Suddenly the infamous dancing girls pranced triumphantly into the classroom, pushing Miss Grundy aside. Then they turned toward the camera and asked, in low, sexy, mellifluous voices, "What do you want, good grammar or good taste?"

Our English teacher, a portly, no-nonsense woman by the name of Mary McGraw, was quick to recognize the failure in logic.

"They assume you're going to take it for granted that you have to choose between good grammar and good taste. But where is it written that you must make that particular choice? No tobacco company is going to trick *my* girls into forgetting how to think analytically. Shoddy grammar is bad enough, but shoddy reasoning is downright dangerous!"

We spent the rest of the class discussing the subtle and not-so-subtle techniques that advertisers use to persuade consumers to do their bidding.

"Take the world's first marketing mogul," said Miss McGraw. "He asked Adam and Eve to choose between a dull, restrictive life devoid of apples, and the freedom to live fully and become like God. I'm surprised they fell for it, aren't you? It's as absurd as being asked to choose between good grammar and good taste. So let's not allow ourselves to be bamboozled by the Winston Fallacy."

The serpent was lucky he didn't have to argue with the tough-minded Miss McGraw. She would stand by the blackboard, chalk in hand, her ample figure looming over us. Good grammar was a tool for clear thinking, she told us, just as accurate mathematical calculations were the *sine qua non* for the construction of safe buildings. Miss McGraw was as enthusiastic in her classroom presentations as the Winston girls were in their TV commercials, although I have difficulty imagining her dancing in a chorus line of grammarphiles.

Nowadays, alas, the love of grammar is all but dead, having been laid to rest by apathy or out-and-out grammarphobia. Miss McGraw would have been shocked. If she were alive today she'd no doubt do her best to rectify the situation, but she would never make the mistake of melting down English grammar to fashion a golden calf. After all, it didn't take her very long to see right through the Winston Fallacy.

And what do *you* want? An invitation to join Miss Grundy for tea at the Association of North American Grammarphiles, or the power to rule the world? But perhaps those aren't the only two choices under the sun. Maybe you can think of some other alternatives that appeal to you more. It's up to you (well, it's partly up to you, anyway).

Work it out with fear and trembling.

Apatrimonio Designs, Aukland, New Zealand

The word *platypus* refers to a creature with flat feet (which is why you hardly ever find them enlisted in the armed services).

THE DUCK-BILLED PLATITUDE

When my daughter, Valerie, was three years old she used to spend countless hours poring over her animal encyclopedia. It was a thick, colorfully illustrated book with pictures of animals ranging from the ordinary to the outlandish. Every night she would ask me to name the creatures that lurked in this book while she stared at them in unblinking fascination. Eventually she discovered the pleasure of being tested on her accumulated knowledge (budding scholar that she was). The two of us would sit cozily on the couch together while she identified the animals that peered at us from the increasingly dog-eared pages of the aging encyclopedia.

It wasn't very long before she invented a game whose rules specified that she didn't have to go to bed until she got an animal wrong. I became a bleary-eyed wreck while she cheerfully waded through the names of hundreds of animals with the accuracy of a key-punch operator (that's what they were doing back then).

"Hah!" I said triumphantly one night. "I'll bet you don't know *this* one!"

"The duck-billed platitude!" she exclaimed, with perfect self-confidence.

It was time for bed.

As I tucked her in I started thinking about how platitudes might relate to our friend the platypus. The first thing that came to mind was the prefix *plat,* which derives from a Greek word meaning *wide,* or *flat*, like a dinner plate. Platitudes, then, are flat statements that lack texture and originality, based on opinions that are not well rounded or fully thought out. The suffix "pus," on the other hand, derives from another Greek word meaning *foot,* like the eight-footed octopus, for example. So the word *platypus* refers to a creature with flat feet (this is why you hardly ever find them enlisted in the armed services).

Here, I felt, was where the similarities ended. The platypus, as we all know, is an aquatic egg-laying mammal with the bill of a duck, the tail of a beaver, and the flat, webbed feet of a waterfowl. Now, it seems to me that God is an expert at creating things that are not platitudes, and if anything is definitely not a platitude, it is the platypus. This shy little guy from Down Under is probably the most original and least platitudinous animal in God's creation.

Are we, as Christians, more like platitudes or platypuses (or *platypi,* or if you prefer)? I think it's fair to say that we are often perceived in hackneyed ways as hypocrites with self-righteous, holier-than-thou attitudes – all of us cut from the same bolt of cloth. Oh, and let's not forget the crutches (useful particularly for the flat-footed among us).

But before we shrug off this distorted image we should admit that there is some truth in platitudes, or they wouldn't be repeated frequently enough to qualify as clichés (from the French word for *stereotyped,* i.e. printed from a solid metal plate). In our desire to avoid being seen as cookie-cutter Christians, we should take care not to become another sort of stereotype, blindly conforming to our culture and thoughtlessly following its trends. We are called upon to be oddballs in the eyes of the world. We are encouraged to be clowns for Christ, which of course was utter foolishness to the rational, sensible Greeks of ancient times.

If you think you look a bit more like a platypus than a wafer-thin Vogue model or a bulging Arnold Schwarzenegger, take heart. Platitudes have a way of reducing unwary targets to the lowest common denominator – a sort of *reductio ad absurdum.*

But we Christians aspire to greater things. We have before us the example of the platypus – a busy, unselfconscious little fellow who breaks all the rules. He is, perhaps, the ultimate biological sketch of everything that is not common, trite or ordinary.

So the next time you hear someone spouting hackneyed truisms and tired clichés, just remember the duck-billed platitude from the southern latitude and adopt an attitude of humble gratitude for the unmerited privilege of being able to live in such an unplatitudinous creation as our incomparable planet Earth.

Photo by Martina Ebel

Was her blind hope really just another form of madness?

MADAME KALEDINA AND THE KINK

When I was a student in Paris I rented a modest room in Montmartre from an elderly White Russian expatriate by the name of Madame Kaledina. She was a well-coifed, tastefully-clad, sensibly-shod woman with a warm smile and intelligent blue eyes.

As time went by she told me how, after a series of dangerous and terrifying adventures, she had managed to escape from the Bolsheviks during the revolution. She had fled her homeland with nothing more than the coat on her back and the equivalent of ten dollars in her pocket. She had lost everything else, including her husband and children, yet she was one of the most cheerful women I had ever met.

"I join my family later," she said, "but right now I am thankful for everythink. I have apartment with view of Sacré-Coeur, I have good job as cleanink lady, and I have Rex," she added, looking fondly at the long-legged Borzoi lying at her feet.

I join my family later. To my young mind those words were a psychological coping mechanism that allowed Madame Kaledina to live with the traumas she had suffered. Her belief in a life everlasting had obviously helped her to fend off loneliness and despair. She had learned to keep up her spirits in spite of the dark horror she must have known in the years before I was born. I admired her for being able to save her sanity by this means, but was her blind hope really just another form of madness?

As the months rolled by our lives settled into a comfortable routine. Every morning I trudged off to the Sorbonne while Madame Kaledina gathered her cleaning materials and her cane and made her way down the Rue St. Vincent to her place of work. I often used to think about her during my lectures. I never did ask her what had caused her lameness, but I assumed that she must have been injured during the Communist revolution. Her left knee was stiff, but I never heard her complain about it.

Our lives were quiet and uneventful until Rex awoke suddenly from his nap one winter evening and looked around the room with an expression of unmistakable alarm. He raised his pointed snout in the direction of his mistress and anxiously sniffed the air. Then, with unaccustomed alacrity, he assembled his long bones into an upright position and gave a sharp, agitated yelp.

Before I could interpret the meaning of this strange behavior he was on his feet and in three ungainly bounds reached Madame Kaledina, who was resting on a chaise longue reading a book. Rex's unexpected arrival was greeted with a little squeal of surprise by his mistress, who then quickly cleared her throat, looking guilty for her outcry. The book fell to the floor, followed by her cane and her reading glasses. The whole situation left her in a state of myopic perplexity.

"Rex, stop that!" she exclaimed, trying to push his head away.

The Borzoi had thrust his wet nose under her skirt and was sniffing her left knee. She gave him a couple of ineffectual taps with her right foot, then leapt from the chaise longue with surprising agility. By the time I reached her side Rex had withdrawn his muzzle and was staring with doleful eyes at his mistress.

"I must call doctor," said Madame Kaledina, reaching for the phone. "Cancer is back. Rex smells it before doctor can make diagnosis. Is thanks to him that first operation was success. He never left my side when cancer was in me. But after operation he settled down. He is good boy, *da?"*

Her second operation was unsuccessful, in spite of Rex's early warning. Madame Kaledina spent her last days gazing out the window at the Sacré-Coeur, stroking the dispirited Borzoi's angular head.

"Do you see how church glows in sprink sun?" she said, her eyes shining. "It is beautifully framed by new buddink leaves." She turned to me as she drew Rex close to her. "I join my family soon, my friend. We will be with Kink."

Her hope no longer seemed like madness to me. Her unshakable serenity and joyful expectation in the face of approaching death made me yearn, for the first time, to know Madame Kaledina's King.

I thank God that today, forty years later, I can pray for all those who have cancer and for the dogs who know it.

Photo by Eric Lawton Photography

My feisty, intrepid mother-in-law, the self-sufficient woman who feared no man, was terrified of a common toad.

TOADAL DEPRAVITY

My mother-in-law is 93 years old and stands about five feet tall in her block-heeled Naturalizer shoes. She is without question a woman to be reckoned with. Nobody scares her, least of all men. She's been a widow for fifty years, and in that time she has developed some firm ideas about the total depravity of God's fallen creation. She's the kind of woman who would make Calvin proud.

Last weekend Gordon and I decided to invite some friends to join us for a picnic lunch at our farm in Lunenburg. I covered the table with a resplendent array of tasty items from the local health food store.

"Forget about health food," my mother-in-law remarked. "I need all the preservatives I can get."

I seated her next to Al Zong, a jovial man whose good-natured character made him the perfect match for her. The two of them hit it off right away.

"I'm Al," he smiled, holding her chair for her. "And what's your name?"

"None of your business," she said tersely. "I'm from New York. I have the right to remain silent."

"No, don't do that," Al replied. "I'd like to hear what you have to say about the meaning of life."

"Figure it out for yourself."

"I was hoping *you* would tell me. Doesn't age bring wisdom?"

"No," she said curtly. "It doesn't bring anything. It comes to the party empty-handed."

For the rest of the picnic lunch Al behaved like a perfect gentleman, impervious to my mother-in-law's volley of caustic comments. He buttered her rolls and cut her chicken off the bone, for which she rewarded him by slapping his wrists and telling him to keep his hands to himself.

"You're flirting with me, aren't you?" she said accusingly.

"What makes you say that?" he asked.

"You're looking guilty, that's why."

"No, I'm not!" he protested.

"Why are you trying to hide it, then?" she shot back. She was in fine fettle that afternoon.

When the meal was over, Al asked her how she took her coffee.

"I like my coffee strong and my men weak," she declared, without missing a beat.

Suddenly she drew in her breath and pointed a trembling finger at the grass nearby. We followed her terrified gaze and saw a rather fat, self-satisfied toad hopping purposefully toward a caterpillar.

"Get him away from here!" she gasped. "*Do* something!"

I stared at her in amazement. My feisty, intrepid mother-in-law, the tough, independent woman who feared no man, was terrified of a common toad.

Al strode confidently over to the offending creature. He scooped him up and came back to the table so the rest of us could have a closer look.

"There's no need to be frightened," he said to my horrified mother-in-law. "They're good for the garden. They eat slugs."

"As far as I'm concerned," she said, "a toad has no redeeming qualities whatsoever."

"He won't bite," Al assured her, holding up the struggling animal for all to admire.

"Get rid of that thing right now," she demanded, "or *I'll* be the one who bites *you*!"

"Do you want me to kill him, then?" Al asked her, giving Gordon a wink.

"Of course not!" cried my mother-in-law. "He's totally disgusting in every conceivable way, but he's a living creature, warts and all!"

"Put him down on the other side of the electric fence," Gordon suggested quietly. Al obediently trudged off in the direction indicated.

"Make sure you wash your hands," my mother-in-law called after him. "And don't come near me till you do. I don't want to get warts."

"Those bumps on his skin aren't contagious," Al said.

"What do *you* know?" she countered.

"You should go and have a little nap, Mom," Gordon suggested. "You look tired."

"Don't tell me what to do," she snapped. "I'm your mother."

Gordon and I exchanged glances, relieved that she was now her old self again after her distressing encounter with one of God's less alluring creatures. We were pleased, too, that she had shown grace and mercy to the hapless toad in spite of his complete unworthiness in her eyes.

Calvin would have been proud indeed.

John N. Schullinger'55 and former patient Valerie Jones'01

"The prognosis for your baby is extremely poor," Dr. Schullinger told us. "The truth is, she's moribund. It would be unfair of me to give you any hope that she'll survive the operation."

The following narrative is the original version of a true story that was later condensed by the Readers Digest, appearing in the August, 1987 edition. This harrowing tale was published in 12 languages and distributed to 15 countries around the world.

WHAT'S WRONG WITH MY BABY?

NEW YORK CITY

APRIL 20TH, 1996: 9:15 AM

It was Parents' Day at Columbia University's College of Physicians and Surgeons. About three hundred professors, medical students and proud parents were milling about in the registration hall. My husband and I were hovering around near the pastry table when I suddenly noticed a slender, silver-haired man serving himself some coffee.

"Gordon!" I cried. "Look over there. It's *him!*"

Before Gordon had a chance to respond I was already bearing down upon my unsuspecting target, who by this time had raised his full cup of coffee to his lips and was about to take a sip.

"Excuse me," I said, as he looked at me over the rim of his cup. "Are you Dr. John Schullinger?"

"Why, yes," he answered, smiling politely but without recognition.

"Please," I said urgently. "Please put your cup down *right now!"*

For a fleeting moment he stared suspiciously at his coffee, as though considering the possibility that it might have been poisoned somehow, then he humbly obeyed my instructions and placed the cup on the table. As soon as I saw that the steaming hot coffee was safely out of the way, I burst into tears and hurled myself into his arms.

"My name is Sonia Jones," I murmured happily into his neck, while his arms dangled by his sides. "I'm the mother of *Valerie* Jones!"

"Oh, my goodness," he said, enfolding me at last in his previously unresponsive arms. "Valerie Jones! I remember that terrible night. It must have been at least twenty or twenty-five years ago…"

WESTCHESTER COUNTY
APRIL 8TH, 1972: 5:00 AM

Gordon and I were suddenly awakened in the pre-dawn hours by a sharp cry from the crib in the corner of the bedroom. It was uncharacteristic of our six-month-old daughter to announce an empty stomach or a soiled diaper with such urgency, so I jumped out of bed to see what was the matter. Just as I was approaching her, Valerie threw up violently and began to cry.

"Projectile vomiting!" I thought, trying hard to recall what Dr. Benjamin Spock had written on the subject. I scooped the baby out of her crib and began pacing the floor, hugging her close. The room was filled with cartons ready to be sent to our new home in Nova Scotia, and hidden somewhere in one of them lay Dr. Spock's book. All I could remember about projectile vomiting was that it could be a prelude to something very serious.

9:15 AM

"Now don't you worry, Mrs. Jones," came the calm voice of Valerie's pediatrician over the phone that morning. "Babies often throw up very hard when they have stomach flu. It's going around, you know, but it's nothing to be concerned about. Just keep giving her liquids and make sure she gets plenty of rest. She'll be fine in a couple of days. But feel free to call me if you have any questions."

The pediatrician had been recommended by a friend of mine who had described him in glowing terms. "He's wonderful with kids," she had said. "And the best thing about him is that he's not an alarmist."

I looked at Valerie with optimistic serenity as I cradled her in my arms, trying my best to emulate the attitude of her totally unalarmed pediatrician. But her expression, which was usually relaxed and happy, reflected a mixture of discomfort and anxiety, and her tiny hands were clenched into fists that appeared to be challenging an unseen danger.

11:00 AM

"The baby is throwing up blood!" I said to the pediatrician over the phone later that morning. I was struggling to sound calm and rational, but the sight of the blood was extremely worrisome to me.

"That's perfectly normal," said the unruffled physician in reassuring tones. "Little babies her age often do that. She has millions of tiny capillaries in her intestinal tract, and it's not unusual for some of them to burst when a baby has a severe case of the flu. Just keep giving her fluids."

"But she doesn't want to nurse any more."

"Well, that's all right, too. After all, when we have the flu we're not usually very hungry, are we?"

1:20 PM

My heart sank when I put Valerie on the changing table and saw traces of blood in her diaper. Could there be so many capillaries bursting that blood would appear from both ends? If it was not unusual for this to happen, as the pediatrician maintained, then why had I never heard other mothers mention it before? Could it be that as a first-time mother I was over-reacting to a situation that was obviously not troubling the pediatrician at all?

"I'm sorry, Mrs. Jones," said a woman's voice when I called his office again. "The doctor has gone to lunch."

"When will he be back?"

"He has a patient at 2:30. Why don't you call at 2:25?"

"But my baby is passing blood in her diapers!"

"I can't help you, Mrs. Jones. I'm only the receptionist. You'll have to talk to the doctor when he returns."

4:00 PM

Valerie was finally admitted to our neighborhood

hospital on the advice of the pediatrician, who said she was a little dehydrated and would show a lot of improvement with the help of some intravenous fluids. The emergency room personnel found it difficult to locate her veins, so they were forced to cut deep gashes in her chubby little ankles to insert the needles. Valerie reacted with admirable stoicism to these painful procedures, refusing to cry in spite of the obvious miseries she had been enduring since the early hours of the morning. Once she was successfully hooked up to a bottle containing the necessary fluids and a prophylactic does of anti-biotics, she was promptly wheeled into the flu ward.

9:00 PM

"*There* she is!" crooned the pediatrician, suddenly appearing next to us in the hospital room. "And how's our little trooper?"

"She's not doing well at all," said Gordon, who had joined me at Valerie's bedside after he came home from work. "My wife tells me she's been throwing up ever since she got here."

"And I still see blood," I added, trying to appear composed.

"I have her on medication that should prevent nausea," said the doctor, placing an avuncular hand on my shoulder. "But I'll have the attending resident put a tube in her stomach to drain the fluids, and that'll give her a chance to get a good night's rest."

"And the blood? What about the *blood?*"

"The capillaries are still acting up, are they?" he said, smiling cheerfully. "Well, the tube will take care of that. When the spasms stop, the capillaries will heal."

"Excuse me doctor," said a nurse in an officious tone of voice. "Visiting hours are over."

"I want you both to go home now and get a good night's sleep," said the pediatrician brightly as he stepped aside to let us pass. "There's nothing you can do for Valerie by sitting here until you're exhausted. She needs her mom and dad to be fresh and rested for her when she checks out tomorrow!"

APRIL 9TH, 1972: 5:30 AM

I awoke to the sound of the phone ringing insistently next to my ear. When I answered, I could hear the sound of the pediatrician's tranquil voice.

"I don't want to alarm you, Mrs. Jones, but I thought it was best for me to be the one to talk to you first. Valerie had a little set-back in the night."

"A set-back?" I echoed, sitting bolt upright.

"It's nothing serious, I assure you," he went on. "She had a bit of a seizure, but it's completely under control now, and she's resting peacefully."

"A *seizure?"* I repeated, feeling the blood rise to my face. "Why?"

"Well, it's quite easy to explain, really. She's been on intravenous fluids since yesterday afternoon and now she's experiencing an imbalance in her blood chemistry. It has to do with her electrolytes, but it's nothing to worry about. It's not unusual for this to happen to small babies like Valerie."

"I want to be with her. I'm coming right away."

"That's fine. But I think I should prepare you for what you'll see. She's looking somewhat… how shall I put it? Somewhat worse for the wear."

"What do you mean?" My heart beat faster.

"During the seizure she managed to scratch herself pretty badly," he explained. "She looks as if she crawled through a briar patch, but the scratches are just superficial. There're no problem at all."

"We're on our way."

"Oh, and Mrs. Jones? I just wanted to warn you that we had to take a few stitches. While she was having the seizure she bit through her lower lip."

4:00 PM

Valerie spent her second day in the hospital in a fitful sleep. She was drowsy, I was told, because of the heavy dose of Phenobarbital that her doctor had prescribed to prevent further seizures. Just to be on the safe side, the nurses had wrapped her wrists in gauze and pinned them to the sheets so she couldn't scratch herself any more.

After staying by her bedside for about two more hours, Gordon had reluctantly gone to work. I spent the rest of the day hounding the long-suffering nurses with interminable questions about Valerie. Were they still taking blood tests to determine the condition of her electrolytes? Why did she seem so restless and uncomfortable in spite of the Pheno-barbital? Why was she so much sicker than the other babies in the flu ward? Was it really so "normal" for babies to scratch and bite themselves during a seizure? How long had the seizure lasted? Who had attended her? *What was wrong with my baby?*

I finally located the resident who was with her when she had suffered the seizure during the night, but he seemed unwilling or unable to describe in detail what had actually happened. It was a seizure, yes. It lasted for around 45 minutes. No, most seizures don't go on for that long. I would have to ask my doctor to explain it to me. That was all he knew.

"Mrs. Jones!" he called after me, as I turned away in frustration.

"Yes?" I said, eager for any information I could wrest from his uncommunicative lips.

"It was awful. I've never seen anything like it. It was just *awful.*"

I felt certain that the resident shot me a warning look as he disappeared down the hall. That glance was to plague me for a long time to come.

7:00 PM

Valerie couldn't seem to get comfortable. She arched her back, pulled up her legs, became rigid, stretched and grimaced. But no matter how much she twisted and turned, she couldn't find a position that satisfied her.

"Do you think we could unpin her wrists?" I asked one of the nurses. "She doesn't seem to like being tied down. Couldn't I have her on my lap? She won't scratch herself if I'm holding her."

The nurse, who by that time had grown tired of my endless questions, decided that I might become less vocal if she let me have my way.

After I had tried for about half an hour to help Valerie feel more comfortable on my lap, I realized that her abdomen had distended quite noticeably within the last ten minutes or so. I wanted to go to the nurses' station to report my findings, but I was sitting in a wheelchair with Valerie and she was hooked up to two separate IVs. There was no way I could get her back to bed without help. I sat there, trapped and terrified, watching her belly continue to grow larger until a nurse finally came into view.

"Yes, Mrs. Jones? What is it *now?*"

"Look at this! Look at the size of her tummy!"

"She's going to have a bowel movement."

"But how can she have a bowel movement when she hasn't eaten anything? Where is it coming from? And how could her abdomen have distended so *quickly?* I don't understand!"

Neither did the nurse, and this made her feel irritated.

"The doctor will answer your questions in the morning, Mrs. Jones."

"But I want to know now. *Right now!*"

"The doctor can't be disturbed," she said, her anger rising. I must have seemed like a child having a tantrum. "He's at *home.* We're not allowed to call him at home."

"*I'll* call him, then. He can't fire *me!* What's his number?"

"I'm sorry, Mrs. Jones, but we can't give out that information."

"Then *you* call him," I pleaded. "If he gets mad at you, just blame it all on me. Tell him I threatened to report him to the Chief of Pediatrics!"

"Mrs. Jones, he *is* the Chief of Pediatrics," she replied as she turned and walked briskly away.

"Then tell him I threatened to call the police!" I called after her. But she was gone.

8:20 PM

Just as I was thinking thoughts that would never qualify me for sainthood, the door burst open and two nurses descended upon me.

"I decided to call the doctor after all," said the first nurse. "He told me to get Valerie down to X-ray immediately."

"No, don't try to get up," the second nurse said. "We're going to take you both down on the wheel-chair, along with the IVs and everything else."

Valerie was taken straight to an X-ray machine. Within a short time a group of doctors, including the pediatrician, had gathered around and were looking at the results on a screen on the wall. Gordon, who had been directed to our location, slipped his hand quietly into mine as we stood listening to what the physicians were saying to one another.

"How could you have missed it?" one of them asked the Chief of Pediatrics. "Why didn't you think about an intussusception?"

"It never occurred to me," he replied, sounding scared. "She didn't fit the statistics. She's a girl, for one thing, and this usually happens to boys. She's only six months old, too, and that puts her on the low end, age-wise. She didn't have cranberry jelly stool, and besides, I didn't know she was in pain. She never even cried! Most kids would have screamed their heads off."

Suddenly the doctors turned around and saw us standing behind them. The pediatrician paled.

"Mr. and Mrs. Jones, there's no time to waste," he said in a trembling voice. "Valerie's life is in the balance. She has to have an operation immediately. If we don't operate, she'll die. It's as simple as that.

It's up to you whether you want my colleague to do it here in this hospital, or whether you want to send her by ambulance to the Columbia Presbyterian Hospital in New York, which is about an hour away. I can't guarantee that she'll live for another hour, but if you want to take a chance on it, I promise you they have the best pediatric surgeons in the world."

"He's absolutely right," said one of the other doctors. "The physicians at Columbia Presbyterian are highly trained specialists, whereas I'm only a general surgeon. I've never operated on a baby before. I have no experience with this sort of thing, but I'll do the best I can if you want me to go ahead with the operation. It's your call, but you have to tell us *at once.*"

There were drops of perspiration on the general surgeon's forehead as he waited for our decision. It was obvious he didn't want Valerie on *his* operating table. I looked at Gordon and I could see right away that we both had the same idea.

"We want the best for our baby," I said. "Send her to the Columbia Presbyterian Hospital. She'll live for another hour. She's a fighter."

"You made exactly the right decision," said the general surgeon, visibly relieved. "I'll go call the ambulance. They'll be here in a matter of minutes."

"You're right about the baby," the pediatrician remarked. "She *is* a fighter. She must be incredibly strong and healthy to have survived this long. This condition is usually fatal after 24 hours, and it's been going on now for what... about 36, 38 hours!"

I felt angry that he took such an impersonal view of the delay, as though it had nothing to do with him. But there was no time for anger.

"Just what exactly *is* her condition, anyway?"

"It's called telescoped bowel, in layman's terms. By some fluke the large intestine caught a piece of the small intestine where the valves meet, and it began sucking it down inside itself by peristalsis."

I stared at him.

"Are you telling me the large bowel *digested* the small bowel?"

"You might say that. Yes, that's it in a nutshell."

"How far down into the large bowel did it go?"

"That's the whole problem, Mrs. Jones. The X-rays show that the small bowel has descended all the way down through the entire large intestinal tract, right down to the sigmoid colon. In other words, almost to the rectum itself."

"Why is her abdomen so big?" I asked, already fearing his answer.

"There's extensive necrosis, I'm afraid. Dead tissue. The digestive fluid from the large bowel has killed the small bowel, you could say. The large bowel has burst, filling the abdominal cavity with infected material. In other words, she has advanced peritonitis. Her abdomen is swollen with gangrene."

10:00 PM

There was no time for panic or tears. The surgeon

had summoned the emergency attendants at about 9:00 PM, only to be informed that the in-house ambulances were not equipped with incubators. The baby had to be kept at body temperature, or she would go into shock. Another decision had to be made: should they operate on the spot, or could we risk an extra hour while a suitable ambulance was sent all the way from Columbia Presbyterian? We decided that Valerie was good for another hour.

By 10:15 the ambulance had still not arrived. Meanwhile the surgeon and the pediatrician had gone home, believing there was nothing more they could do. I accosted a passing resident and told him what was happening. He took pity on us and sat down by a phone, dialing numbers until he finally discovered that the ambulance driver, who was from Chicago, had lost his way. The resident remained on the line with the driver, explaining step-by-step how to get to our hospital while we waited with our hearts in our mouths.

At 10:35 the ambulance paramedics came running down the corridor and were quickly taken to the intensive care unit. Suddenly the two men came to an abrupt halt and stared at Valerie as she lay fighting for her life.

"What's *that?"* one of them exclaimed.

"That's the *baby!"* I cried, barely able to contain my impatience. "What are you waiting for? Get her to the ambulance right *now*!"

"We can't," said the other man.

"What do you mean?" Gordon demanded.

"We were told she was an *infant.* We assumed they meant a premature baby. This child is much too big for the incubator!"

"You'll just have to stuff her in anyway. Let her legs hang out. Whatever. Come on, *get going!* She could die any minute!"

The paramedics careened down the hall again, pushing Valerie in her regular incubator to the emergency dock where the ambulance was waiting.

While they were stuffing her into the smaller incubator inside the ambulance, I hopped into the vehicle and settled myself on a bench.

"What do you think you're doing?" said one of the paramedics.

"I'm going with you."

"No you're not," he shouted, pulling my arm. "It's against regulations."

"You'll get lost again if I don't come along," I protested, digging in my heels and holding onto a bar on the wall. "Let's go! We don't have any time to lose!"

"All right," he relented. "But if the baby starts to fail, we may have to resuscitate her. We may have to bang her chest real hard. So I'm warning you, lady, if you interfere with us I'll knock you out. Do you understand me?"

"It's a deal. Let's go!"

"I've got a witness," he barked, pointing to his partner.

"Go! *Go!* GO!!!" I cried.

We left the emergency dock on two wheels, the siren wailing in the night, with Gordon following directly behind us in our small Volkswagen.

APRIL 10TH, 1972: 12:10 AM

As the paramedics deftly wheeled Valerie into the ER at Columbia Presbyterian, the admitting nurse looked over her glasses at the little legs protruding from the incubator and asked an all-too-familiar question.

"What's *that?"* she said, looking perplexed.

"That's my daughter, and she's bursting with gangrene. She needs an operation *RIGHT THIS MINUTE!"*

I couldn't understand how two different people could become frozen like statues at the sight of my desperately ill baby.

"Nobody told us that it was an *infant!* We were expecting an adult."

"Well, so what?" I exclaimed, at my wit's end. "What's the difference?"

"The point," the nurse said evenly, "is that we heated the adult operating theater for this patient. Now we'll have to heat up the *pediatric* operating room."

"And how long will *that* take?" I demanded, unable to lower my voice.

"Oh, about an hour," she replied, looking totally unperturbed.

1:00 AM

Gordon and I were taken to a waiting room in the bowels of the Babies Hospital of the Columbia Presbyterian Medical Center, where we waited for what seemed like an eternity for the pediatric surgeon to come and talk to us. Finally a handsome young man with blue eyes and blond hair came toward us with a clipboard in his hand.

"This can't be the surgeon," I thought. "They must have sent a medical student."

"Mr. and Mrs. Jones?" said the fair-haired boy, approaching us with his hand extended. "I'm Dr. John Schullinger. I'm going to operate on your baby in just a few minutes, but I wanted to have a word with you first. We don't have much time, so I hope you'll forgive me if I come straight to the point. The prognosis for your baby is extremely poor. The truth is, she's moribund. It would be unfair of me to give you any hope that she'll survive the operation. If she does live, she could very well suffer serious brain damage. I'm deeply sorry to have to be the one to bring you this news, but you have every right to know the facts. And now, if you'll excuse me, I must go. Every minute counts. I'll come back after the operation, and we'll talk as long as you like."

There is something visceral about the relationship between a mother and her baby. I felt nauseated by Dr. Schullinger's chilling news, and profoundly distressed by the fact that I was completely helpless in this situation. How much experience could this boy surgeon have, anyway? I sat on the bench in the waiting room and cried inconsolably, until I heard Gordon's words in my ear.

"Stop," he was saying, in a pleading voice. "I can't stand it! You must stop crying."

Grief is a feeling that is hard to share, even with loved ones. Gordon seemed to be in another world, far away and out of reach. Even his words had an unreal quality, as though I were being anesthetized. I felt walled in by a cocoon of pain and hollow silence. I could do nothing to comfort Gordon from inside my personal isolation ward. The only thing I could do for him was to stop crying.

I'm ashamed to say that I prayed to God for the first time that night. Like many other supposedly self-sufficient people, I waited until I was overcome with grief and helplessness before it occurred to me to turn to him for help. I had often heard it said that

God is merciful, and that he is, in fact, love itself. Those words came to life for me that night in the barren, silent waiting room, a room that must have witnessed the bitter tears of countless other parents over the years.

7:00 AM

I had peeked out the door of the waiting room many times during the night, wishing there were someone I could talk to about how the operation was going, but the halls were dark and the nurses' station was empty. It seemed as if we were in a wing of the hospital that hadn't been used in years.

Just as Gordon and I were beginning to wonder if we should be devising a plan of action, I heard the tell-tale squeak of crepe soles coming along the hall. When I opened the door I saw a nurse preparing to put her shoulder bag down on the desk. I quickly ran up to her.

"Could you please call the operating room and find out how my baby is?" I cried out breathlessly as I approached her.

She looked at me with curiosity for a moment, then calmly continued to divest herself of her many belongings.

"Do you mind if I take off my coat first?" she asked, with a hint of sarcasm.

"Yes, I do mind. I mind *terribly!*"

She looked me up and down with the kind of expression that implied years of experience listening to the hyperbole of distraught mothers.

"All right, already!" she said wearily, picking up the receiver and dialing a number. "What's the name of the patient?"

"Valerie Jones."

"And the surgeon?"

"Dr. John Schullinger."

"Dr. Schullinger?" she repeated. "Then you have no worries. He's a very famous surgeon. He's the best there is. I'm sure your baby is doing just fine."

"No, you don't understand! He told me last night that he didn't think she'd make it! He said she was *moribund!*"

The nurse nodded and held up her hand to silence me as she spoke to someone on the other end of the line.

"Yeah," she said. "I tried to tell her, but she wouldn't believe me."

"What?" I cried, tugging at her sleeve. "What are they saying?"

Sudden waves of hope came flooding over me. Gordon's eyes were misty.

"Like I said, she's doing just fine," the nurse said in a matter-of-fact tone of voice as she replaced the receiver. "She's in the intensive care unit now. Dr. Schullinger is just washing up. He'll be here soon to talk to you. I told you, he's a very famous surgeon. He doesn't lose babies."

NEW YORK CITY
APRIL 20TH, 1996: 1:30 PM

When I finally got around to reading the agenda for the Parents' Day program at Columbia's College of Physicians and Surgeons, I was surprised to find that the luncheon speaker was none other than Dr. John Schullinger. I approached the professor who was chairing the program and asked her if I could make an impromptu speech before Dr. Schullinger addressed the audience.

She looked at me dubiously, wondering what to make of this unusual request. But when I told her what I wanted to say, she agreed to let me take the microphone at the appropriate moment.

"So in conclusion," I said to the smiling parents, after briefly explaining what had happened on that unforgettable night 24 years ago, "I'm delighted to have this opportunity to thank Dr. Schullinger for making it possible for Gordon and me to be here on this occasion as the parents of an incoming student. I know now that God was surely guiding his hand that night. Who could have ever predicted that our daughter would end up being mentored by the very man who saved her life so many years ago? I would also like to thank Columbia's administrators for devising such a brilliant early-identification system, for in retrospect it has become obvious to me that here at the College of Physicians and Surgeons you save babies so you can train them later on to be doctors who in turn will save *other* babies. Isn't this, after all, what medicine is all about?"

Valerie Jones received her BA from Dalhousie University in Nova Scotia and a Master's in Biblical Studies from the Dallas Theological Seminary. She completed her pre-med requirements at Calvin College, and then participated in a genetic research project at the Mayo Clinic. She received her MD from the College of Physicians and Surgeons at Columbia University, and completed her residency in rehabilitation medicine at St. Vincent's Hospital in New York City. She is now the Senior Medical Director at Revolution Health in Washington, DC.

Although Valerie's entire large intestine and much of the small bowel were resected, the skill of her pediatric surgeon was such that she has lived until now without symptoms.

If you enjoyed reading *Of Mice and Moose Calls,* you will also like *It All Began With Daisy* (Dutton/Penguin, New York, 1987), about Sonia's life on a farm in Nova Scotia, where she and her husband Gordon parlayed their Jersey cow into a multimillion dollar yogurt industry.

You can purchase a brand new hardcover first edition at **www.erserandpond.com**, or you may send a check or money order for $25.95 (please add $2.16 for sales tax plus $6.00 for postage and handling) to Erser and Pond Ltd, 1096 Queen St, Suite 225, Halifax, Nova Scotia B3H 2R9, Canada. Checks and money orders should be made out to Erser and Pond. If you would like a personal autograph by Sonia Jones, please press the "contact us" button on the website and indicate the name of the person to whom the book should be inscribed.

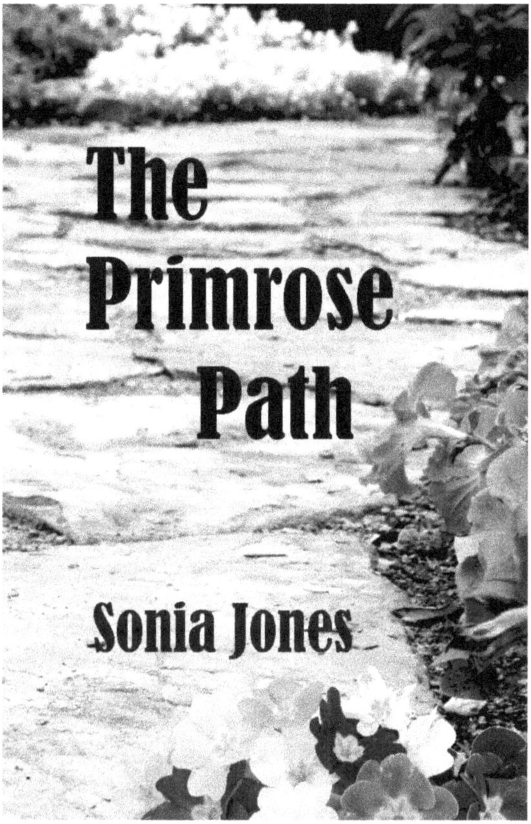

If you enjoyed reading *Of Mice and Moose Calls,* you will also like *The Primrose Path* (Erser and Pond, 2008). This true story touches on Percy Pond, the author's grandfather and celebrated frontier photographer who documented the Klondike Gold Rush, the founding of Juneau, and the culture of the native tribes in Alaska. It also introduces Kay Harrison, the author's charismatic father, who was the Managing Director of Hollywood's Technicolor Films in Paris, London, and Rome.

You can get a brand new first edition at **www.erserandpond.com**, or you may send a check or money order for $19.95 (please add $2.16 for sales tax plus $4.00 for postage and handling) to Erser and Pond Ltd, 1096 Queen St, Suite 225, Halifax, Nova Scotia B3H 2R9, Canada. Checks and money orders should be made out to Erser and Pond Ltd.

The
PENINSULA FARM
YOGOURT
COOKBOOK
by Sonia Jones

www.ingramcontent.com/pod-product-compliance
Lightning Source LLC
Chambersburg PA
CBHW061943070426
42450CB00007BA/1033
9780981047003